MARCO

BULGARIA

POLAND UKRAINE
SLOVAKIA
                        MOLD
       Budapest   OVA
HUNGARY   ROMANIA
CROATIA
                Bucharest   Black
BOSNIA Belgrade   Sea
HERZEG. SERBIA
              BULGARIA
    MNE KOSOVO Sofia
         MACE
    ALBA- DONIA
    NIA   TURKEY
       GREECE

← INSIDE FRONT COVER:
THE BEST HIGHLIGHTS

The best Insider Tips → p. 4

INSIDER TIP

Best of ... → p. 6

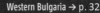

Western Bulgaria → p. 32

Central Bulgaria → p. 56

SYMBOLS

INSIDER TIP ▶ Insider-Tip

★   Highlight

●●●●   Best of ...

🔆   Scenic view

😊   Responsible travel: fair
trade principles and the
environment respected

(*)   Telephone numbers
that are not toll-free

PRICE CATEGORIES HOTELS

Expensive	over 120 lv
Moderate	80 – 120 lv
Budget	under 80 lv

Prices are for two people sharing a double room per night,
breakfast included

PRICE CATEGORIES RESTAURANTS

Expensive	over 35 lv
Moderate	20 – 35 lv
Budget	under 20 lv

Prices are for a meal with
starter, main course and dessert, including drinks

On the cover: Bulgarian art in Rila Monastery p. 41 | Melnik's famous red wine p. 42

CONTENTS

Northeastern Bulgaria → p. 72

Black Sea Coast → p. 80

Trips & Tours → p. 94

Road atlas → p. 122

MAPS IN THE GUIDEBOOK
(124 A1) Page numbers and
coordinates refer to the road
atlas
(0) Site/address located off
the map. Coordinates are
also given for places that are
not marked on the road atlas
(U A1) Refers to the map of
Sofia inside the back cover

**INSIDE BACK COVER:
PULL-OUT MAP →**

PULL-OUT MAP 𝄞
(𝄞 A–B 2–3) Refers to the
removable pull-out map
(𝄞 a–b 2–3) Refers to addi-
tional inset maps on the
pull-out map

The best MARCO POLO Insider Tips

Our top 15 Insider Tips

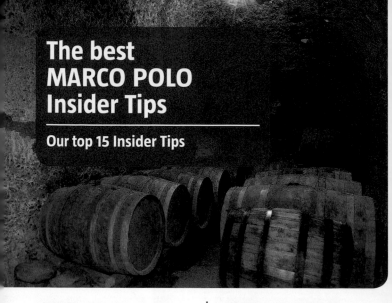

INSIDER TIP **Jesus in a space ship**
How bizarre! Two icons in the 17th-century St Theodor church in the village of Dobarsko show Jesus Christ taking off in a rocket. For many years, locals and scientists have been seeking an explanation for this unusual image → **p. 38**

INSIDER TIP **History in stone and wood**
The houses look as if they've been made for a film set. And in fact several films have actually been shot in the museum villages of Kovachevitsa and Leshten in the western Rhodopes → **p. 63**

INSIDER TIP **Orpheus and Eurydice**
Legend has it that Orpheus, the most famous singer in antiquity, descended from the Trigradsko Zhdrelo Gorge into the underworld in search of his beloved Eurydice. He set off on his dangerous journey from the Devil's Throat cave in the Rhodopes → **p. 64**

INSIDER TIP **Fortified overview**
Enjoying a unique location and view, the Asenova Krepost fortress protected the road through the Rhodopes during the Middle Ages → **p. 62**

INSIDER TIP **Art treasures in the labyrinth**
In the Magura dripstone cave, Bronze Age artists depicted wild animals and fertility symbols, using bat droppings for paint → **p. 55**

INSIDER TIP **Stylish dining in a traditional setting**
Dine in one of the finest houses in Veliko Tarnovo, the Hadji Nikoli Tavern, the former home of a wealthy 19th-century merchant → **p. 68**

INSIDER TIP **A kaleidoscope of flashing lights**
Bulgaria's history is symbolically portrayed in Veliko Tarnovo through a powerful son et lumière show. A treat for the senses → **p. 68**

INSIDER TIP Picturesque museum villages

Time has stood still in Bozhentsi. Wells, houses and artisans' shops look now just as they did 150 years ago → **p. 70**

INSIDER TIP Al fresco weddings

You may catch sight of a Christian Orthodox wedding ceremony in Lovers' Alley in the grounds of the former royal summer residence (photo below) in Balchik → **p. 92**

INSIDER TIP Rocky coastline

Thracian tombs, breathtaking cliff landscapes, an abandoned cave town – in antiquity people lived in what is now the Jailata Nature Reserve near Kamen Bryag → **p. 93**

INSIDER TIP Monastery walk

Sveta Troitsa near Veliko Tarnovo is situated on a rocky slope in the Jantra Gorge and is only accessible on foot → **p. 103**

INSIDER TIP Casks that pack a punch

The wine cellar for Kordopulov House in Melnik, formerly owned by a wine merchant, was built directly into the cliffs (photo left) → **p. 42**

INSIDER TIP A romantic seaside setting

The stunningly beautiful Irakli beach, with its sparkling, crystal clear water, forms part of a nature reserve → **p. 99**

INSIDER TIP From the sea straight into the pot

The Dalboka restaurant near Cape Kaliakra serves every conceivable type of mussel. The shellfish are farmed in the offshore beds opposite → **p. 93**

INSIDER TIP Dancing on glowing coals

This ancient, mystical rite is performed on St Constantine and St Elena's Day. How the dancers never burn their feet remains a mystery → **p. 107**

BEST OF ...

FOR FREE

● *Natural spectacle by Lake Durankulak*
Save yourself a visit to the zoo and go to Lake *Durankulak,* an important over-wintering area for migratory birds, and in particular thousands of red-breasted geese. Also ferruginous ducks, marsh harriers, cormorants and white pelicans – and not only in winter (photo) → **p. 92**

● *Barbecue overlooking the Black Sea*
You have to bring your own meat with you, but the fire and the view of the Black Sea are free. A natural gas fire has been burning on the edge of *Kamen Bryag* since the end of the 1950s; locals and visitors love to come and picnic here → **p. 93**

● *Acoustic delights in the cathedral*
On Sundays and religious holidays go and listen to the choir during the church service in the *St Alexander Nevski Cathedral in Sofia*. It's one of the finest 20th-century buildings in the Balkans and you don't have to pay a penny to see it → **p. 49**

● *Archaeological treasures in the subway*
You can inspect and admire ancient artefacts in a museum – or for free in the *Serdika* pedestrian subway in Sofia. View also the remains of the Serdika fortress, which was built in the 2nd century by the Roman emperors Marcus Aurelius and Commodus → **p. 44**

● *Bell-ringing concert in Bansko*
Seven bells ring out from the *Sveta Troitsa* church tower in Bansko. Stand outside and hear the concert free of charge. On Saturdays, Sundays and religious holidays, the bell ringers play tunes only ever heard in Bansko → **p. 36**

● *International Jazz Festival*
The International Jazz Festival is held in Bansko every year from 8 to 13 August. You can listen to outstanding musicians and meet fans from all over the world. And the best thing about it is that admission to the concerts on the central square is free → **p. 107**

○○○○ Dots in guidebook refer to 'Best of ...' tips

● *The sounds of Pirin*
Melodies, passionate singers, traditional instruments – in the *Mehana Vodenitsata* in Bansko you can listen to members of Banski Starcheta, a male voice choir, performing music from the Pirin Mountains and watch locals dance the horo → **p. 37**

● *Cheverme – lamb kebab*
To make a *cheverme,* the lamb roast has to be turned above the fire for at least seven hours. Sample the dish at traditional festivals and also in certain restaurants such as *Chevermeto* in Nessebar where the *cheverme* is spit roasted in the dining room before the customers' very own eyes → **p. 84**

● *Sozopol – it could be by the Mediterranean*
Soak up the Mediterranean atmosphere in *Sozopol,* a picturesque little town on the Black Sea coast, and enjoy a walk through its labyrinth of delightful narrow streets. Fig trees flourish in the inner courtyards, there's a whiff of dried fish and the sea is visible from all over the town (photo) → **p. 85**

● *Rila monastery can boast some splendid architecture*
From the outside it's a medieval fortress, from the inside it's richly decorated with attractive architectural features and colourful ornamentation. If you want to find out about Bulgarian culture and architecture, do not miss *Rila Monastery*, an important Orthodox monastery and Unesco World Heritage Site → **p. 41**

● *The high peaks of Bulgaria*
Rocky mountains, green slopes, blue lakes – the quintessential Bulgarian countryside in the *Rila Mountains* is for everyone to enjoy. The quickest way to get there is via Borovec and then on the chairlift to the Jastrebec mountain hut. Admire the view of Musala, the highest peak on the Balkan peninsula → **p. 40**

● *The source of perfume*
Give your senses a real treat: *rose oil* is Bulgaria's top export. It's extracted in Rose Valley where the air is heavy with fragrance when the flowers bloom and the petals are harvested. You can also buy rose oil as a souvenir throughout the country, in Sofia, from the TSUM department store → **p. 50**

ONLY IN

BEST OF ...

● *Explore Plovdiv's past*
In Plovdiv Old Town, visit the well-preserved houses dating from the so-called Revival period and look out in particular for the furnishings. The interior furniture and decoration of the *Nedkovich House* is magnificent, especially in the ladies' salon (photo) → **p. 60**

● *Cave visit in the rain*
Wet weather adds to the spectacle! Descend into Bulgaria's labyrinthine caverns and admire the spectacle of an underground waterfall in *Djavolkso Garlo* → **p. 64**

● *Thracian gold in Sofia*
In central Bulgaria scientists discovered some 15,000 items of gold, mainly jewellery, made by the ancient Thracians. Admire these treasures and many other centuries-old exhibits in the *National Museum of History* in Sofia → **p. 46**

● *Opera trumps bad weather*
Famous Bulgarian opera singers appear on stages all over the world. So go and listen to the wonderful voices of the emerging young talent at the *Opera House* in Sofia → **p. 36**

● *Iconic art in Bulgarian Orthodox churches*
The Bulgarian Orthodox churches are famous for their icons, which in many places have been magnificently restored. The painted-wood representations of saints and biblical scenes are unusual and delightful, e.g. in *Boyana church* → **p. 52**

● *By train through the Balkans*
Travel in a rain-free railway carriage past forests and gorges, through villages and meadows – the *Rhodope railway* is the last remaining narrow gauge railway operating in Bulgaria. Take a relaxing five-hour trip through the wild Pirin and Rhodope Mountains → **p. 97**

RAIN

RELAX AND CHILL OUT
Take it easy and spoil yourself

● *Wine tasting in a regal setting*
A summer terrace with a view of the Black Sea, next to you the rotating wheel of an old water mill, in your hand a glass of wine from the Regina collection ... enjoy a wine tasting session at the *Queen's Wine House* in Dvoretsa in Balchik → **p. 92**

● *By lift for a panoramic view over Sofia*
Take a gentle ride on the gondola lift from Simeonovo to the heart of the *Vitosha Mountains* and you'll have the whole of Sofia at your feet→ **p. 53**

● *Coffee culture*
Enjoy a totally relaxing start to the day over a cup of coffee, pause for a moment to make your plans and have a chat with the locals – e.g. in the *Flocafe Lounge Bar* in Sofia. Situated in the city centre, this modern coffee house has smart furniture and serves various blends → **p. 49**

● *A taste of sun and sea on a yacht*
Find a skipper, e.g. on the 'Aurora', to take you on a gentle cruise around *Balchik* Bay and enjoy both the view and the soothing motion of the waves. A picnic on the beach will round off the perfect day → **p. 92**

● *Sunset at Cape Kaliakra*
The only place in Bulgaria where you can watch the sun set over the Black Sea is at *Cape Kaliakra* (photo) → **p. 93**

● *Alone on the beach*
Relax in the sun, alone, on a deserted beach – you can do this, high up in the north at *Kosmos Camping*, 6km/4mi from the Bulgarian-Romanian border → **p. 98**

● *Medicinal waters*
Spa hotels in Bulgaria provide a whole range of wellness treatments and in many places hot water gurgles up out of the ground. Paddle in pools of mineral water at the *Medite Hotel* in Sandanski → **p. 38**

INTRODUCTION

DISCOVER BULGARIA!

Fine beaches and austere mountains, unspoilt hilltop villages and lively major towns, effervescent temperament and Mediterranean laissez-faire – all this makes Bulgaria a country of contrasts, a delightful mix of east and west. The travel catalogues are full of sea and beach, in other words the Black Sea coast – a beautiful and important part of the country. But if you stick to the tourists trails, you'll miss out on what's really worth seeing.

Mother nature has been very kind to Bulgaria. With its surface area of a little under 43,000sq.mi, it's not a particularly large country (England measures just over 50,000sq.mi), but it has to a great extent been richly endowed with diversity and beautiful scenery, with mountains and a coast measuring 378km/235mi, and it's densely wooded with many lakes. In other words, Bulgaria has something for everyone: for beach lovers a holiday by the Black Sea; for skiers the ski runs around Bansko, for hikers and bikers the green peaks of the Rila and Pirin Mountains; and if you're looking for solitude, you'll find it by hidden mountain lakes. To all of this add any

Photo: Belogradchik Rocks south of Vidin in Western Bulgaria

In the glorious morning sun the Golden Sands live up to their name

amount of culture in the world-famous monasteries and the picturesque, beautifully restored villages.

In terms of geography and culture, Bulgaria is a point of transition between Europe and the Orient, a fact which has also shaped its history and society. So it's no wonder that although relatively small, it is home to nine sites which have acquired Unesco World Heritage status: Rila Monastery, Nessebar, the Kazanlak Tomb, the Thracian Tomb of Sveshtari, the Horseman of Madara, Boyana Church, Ivanovo Rock-hewn Churches, Pirin National Park and the Srebarna Nature Reserve.

Point of transition between Europe and the Orient

681–1018
First Bulgarian Empire; huge expansion under Simeon I

863
First Slavic alphabet, founding of the standard Slav written language by the monks Cyril and Methodius

865
Christianity adopted

1018–1185
Byzantine rule

1185–1396
Second Bulgarian Empire

1396–1878
Ottoman rule, Christians subject to the Patriarchate of Constantinople

It was the Black Sea coast which really made the country well known as a tourist destination, with its austere and rocky north, the large coastal resorts in and around Varna and the fine-grained beaches at Golden Sands. In some coastal regions, the foothills of the Balkan Mountains with their luxuriant vineyards reach down almost to the sea. In the country's interior, there are lots of national parks (e.g. Pirin) which seek to reconcile environmental protection with sustainable tourism. But it's often the case that communities are forced to make a choice between environmental protection and business.

Life on the coast is colourful, especially in the summer, with the locals and tourists celebrating exuberantly in pubs and bars. But in spite of some manifestations of excessive drinking, which can be found in the large hotel complexes, the Bulgarians continue to place great value on all aspects of their history and culture. Visitors will probably not have a single conversation with a native Bulgarian in which the 'yoke' of almost 500 years of Ottoman foreign rule is not mentioned. And their pride in Bulgarian culture, free of all foreign influences, is all the greater. Their roots go back to the time before the 15th century and from the middle of the 19th century. In an idiosyncratic interpretation of history, they refer to the great empires of the tsars and the movement of National Revival, of which the latter especially has left the country with impressive cultural monuments.

The world-famous monasteries are worth a visit in their own right. They are an expression of a unique combination of nature, culture, religion and history, and their function has always extended beyond matters of church and religion. Not only the Slav alphabet – foundation of the Cyrillic script –, but important schools of literature, ar-

From 1762
'National Revival': striving for cultural and religious independence; from the middle of the 19th century a national revolutionary movement is formed

1876–1878
National movement's April Uprising is brutally suppressed (1876); Russo-Turkish War (1877–78)

1878
Bulgaria gains independence, one part remaining under Ottoman sovereignty

1879
First democratic constitution, Bulgaria becoming a principality

chitecture and the visual arts can trace their origins back to the monasteries. Thus visitors on their tour of the religious sites will find themselves wandering through nine centuries of Bulgaria's spiritual, political and cultural history. Several monasteries also offer overnight accommodation.

Whole towns and villages enjoy protected status

The second jewel in the crown of the country's cultural diversity takes us back to the time of the National Revival. Almost everywhere in the country you can't help but bump into restored 19th-century houses. In some regions whole towns and villages enjoy protected status, especially in Central Bulgaria. In the area around Veliko Tarnovo, for example, there's the merchants' village of Arbanasi (17th century) which must be singled out above all, or Koprivshtitsa, a picturesque village between Sofia and Plovdiv. Then, in Nessebar and Sozopol by the Black Sea, there are veritable gems of the art of woodcarving dating from the Revival architecture.

The third and final highlight is the landscape. The Balkans, a word coming from the Turkish meaning 'forested mountain', lends its name to a whole region. There are also the Rila Mountains in the southwest and the Rhodopes in the south, which bestride the whole country from east to west and whose high peaks are especially well suited for longer hikes and also climbing tours.

Improvisation is the magic word in the Balkans

However, all these treasures cannot conceal the country's problems. Like many eastern European countries, Bulgaria also has to struggle with high rates of unemployment, a lack of sales markets, considerable environmental damage and a huge black economy. People try to help themselves by strengthening family ties and with imaginative improvisation, the magic word in the Balkans, convert their garage into a hen house or use it for growing mushrooms; not a few set themselves up as fortune tellers by the roadside or offer the services of an ancient pair of scales as a means of weight control. But it has to be said that such measures cannot in the long run improve the economic situation

1887
Prince Ferdinand of Saxo-Coburg and Gotha becomes Prince of Bulgaria

1908
Prince Ferdinand declares the independence of both parts of Bulgaria. The country again becomes a tsardom

1912–1913
Balkan Wars

1918
Tsar Boris III (until 1943)

1941
Entry into the Second World War on the German side. The royal house and the general population successfully resist the persecution and deportation of the Jews living in the country

In the background, the impressive St Alexander Nevski Cathedral in Sofia

of many people. Many younger people within the total population of about 7.5 million are therefore looking to leave and settle somewhere in western Europe or overseas. Most Bulgarians are sooner or later disappointed by politicians of all colours, as is shown by the regular changes of government which is no wonder, when the needs of the many are getting no less whilst corruption flourishes, irrespective of whichever government is in power. The Bulgarians have always placed great value on their belonging to the European cultural tradition and since 2007 the country has been a member of the EU, to the delight of the inhabitants – who are also pleased with the financial help which is now flowing in from Brussels.

And yet, despite all these adverse circumstances, at the first signs of spring the country and its people really start to blossom again. The sun radiates tangible optimism. The Bulgarians' much praised sociability emerges from the living room out onto the streets and into the numerous bars. And hospitality seems to be quite inexhaustible in this beautiful country. Come and discover it for yourself!

1944
Soviet troops occupy the country

1946
Bulgaria is declared a People's Republic

1989
End of one party rule

1990
First free elections in more than 50 years

2004
Membership of Nato

2007
Bulgaria becomes a member of the EU

2009
The centre-right GERB becomes the party of government

WHAT'S HOT

1 Bulgarian wine

Swirl, sniff, taste Wine is the most fashionable drink amongst Bulgarians and, as they like to show their commitment to their home country, they drink Bulgarian wine. But it's not just the patriots who enjoy its taste. The *Tauri cellar (76.12.21.227:8084)* grows its own grapes in Targovishte and enjoys a good reputation. If you'd like to see a wide selection of local wines, then you should visit the *Trovatore Wine Bar (Ulitsa Midjur 23, Sofia)*. In the *Enoteca Uno* you can eat really well and in the cellar there will be the perfect wine to complement your meal *(Bulevard Vassil Levski 45, Sofia)*.

East meets west 2

Creative The contemporary artists who exhibit in Sofia's *Lessedra Art Gallery* come from all over the world to exchange ideas with their Bulgarian colleagues *(Ulitsa Milin Kamak 25)*. Aspiring talents such as Onnik Karanfilian *(photo)* get their chance in the *Rakursi Gallery (Ulitsa Han Krum 4a)*. One name worth making a note of is Elisaveta Aleksandrova. Her trademark is pop portraits *(www.meaus.com/93-aleksandrova.htm)*.

Smart & stylish

3

Fashion The classic look is back in fashion. After a few years in the wilderness, Bulgarian designers are turning their backs on the eccentric. The latest styles are again featuring classic cuts, timeless elegance and top-quality fabrics. But that doesn't have to mean boring – just have a look at *Caspasca (Bulevard Vitosha 60, Sofia)*. The creations by Evgenia Zhivkov *(Bulevard Patriarch Evtimij 12, Sofia)* are wonderfully feminine, and elegance is the name of the game at *Markram (Bulevard Vladislav Varnenchik 136, Varna, photo)*. All the matching accessories are available at *Dizi (Ulitsa Zhelezarksa 22, Plovdiv)*.

Open Sesame

Soviet nostalgia Bulgaria is now looking back over its totalltarian past. In the autumn of 2011 the first museum for socialist art was opened in Sofia, showing busts of Lenin and co., propaganda paintings and a sculpture garden with works dating from 1944–89 *(Ulitsa Lachezar Stanchev)*. In Sofia there's a restaurant which thrives on those ambivalent memories. The tiny *Gara za Dvama* is modelled on an old train and serves authentic home cooking; the sibirski pelmeni (dumplings filled with meat) are highly recommended *(Ulitsa Benkovski 18)*. You can enjoy an after-dinner walk with *Bulgaria Communism Tours*, a company which also offers multi-day excursions in Soviet-era style – from vehicle to accommodation *(bulgaria-communismtours.com, photo)*.

All aboard

Snowboarding Bulgaria is still not very well-known as a winter sport destination but the snow and reasonable prices are a magical attraction for boarders. Facilities are good throughout the Rhodopes, but especially in the unspoilt village of Momchilovtsi, where enthusiasts will find a purpose-built snowboard park *(www.bulgaria ski.com)*. Since the 1970s businesses in Borovets have been successfully working together to create a modern ski resort with high-quality facilities – and now boarders also come from abroad. The *Ice Angels* hotel aims to provide winter sport fans with professional training and support *(Borovets, www. iceangelshotel.com)*. If you're still not sure about the quality of the Bulgarian pistes, then René Eckert's snowboarding documentary 'At Equilibrium' may well make you change your mind *(high definition download at http://vimeo.com/14538620, photo)*.

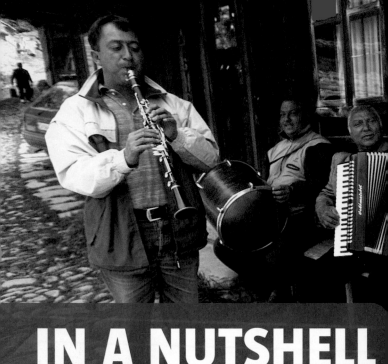

IN A NUTSHELL

COSMETICS FROM ROSE OIL

Rose oil is perhaps Bulgaria's best-known export. The precious ethereal oil is extracted from the petals of the Damask Rose and it is Bulgaria's oldest industry, now accounting for about 70% of the world's total rose oil production. You can buy it in small wooden containers as a souvenir throughout the country. In recent years, however, cosmetic products have also been developed using rose oil. Face creams, rose water, perfumes, soaps and even scented candles are sold in many places in the country, not only in the famous Rose Valley.

CYRIL AND METHODIUS

The brothers Cyril (originally Konstan-tin, born 826 or 827, died 869) and Methodius (born around 815, died 885), in the west generally known by the name 'Apostles of the Slavs', are the founders of the Slav alphabet (Glagolitic script) and Slav written language and literature. They were born in Saloniki (modern day Thessaloniki) and educated in Byzantium. At the request of the Moravian Prince Rostislaw, they were sent by the Byzantine Emperor Michael III to Moravia to teach Christian beliefs to the Slavs living there, using their mother tongue, and at the same time to combat Franco-German influences. Shortly after the Glagolitic script was devised, another system of writing was established which was used to transcribe ancient Slav texts, receiving the name 'Cyrillic', though this name did not

Photo: Musicians outside a Revival House

Music and dance, a stunning world of nature and world-famous monasteries – tradition and joie de vivre all add to Bulgaria's appeal

come from Cyril himself. The Bulgarians' admiration for the two 'Apostles of the Slavs' has survived through all the different political systems to the present. The 'National Day of Culture' (also popularly known as the 'Cyrillic Alphabet Day') is held on 24 May, which was previously the 'Day of the two Saints' but, based on the church calendar, that now falls on 11 May.

FLORA AND FAUNA

Bulgaria has two faces: the luxuriant green with the numerous fields and plan-tations in full bloom on the fertile soil, and then the barren, scorched brown of late summer when the country pays its dues to the sun. The world of animals and plants is also indicative of Bulgaria's border and transitional character. To the north of the Balkans and in the mountain regions there's a predominance of central European vegetation. The south, on the other hand, is more Mediterra-nean with olive trees, myrtle, cypresses and evergreen oak. About a third of the country is wooded, 25 percent of which

Cyril and Methodius
founded the Slav alphabet

had a terrible effect on fish stocks in the Black Sea. Seals and dolphins are almost extinct and even the turbot is endangered. The freshwater rivers and lakes are mainly home to trout and carp. Bulgaria lies on the Via Pontica, an ancient Roman road along the Black Sea heavily used by migrating birds. More than 110 species of birds fly this way twice a year, including 30 different birds of prey, pelicans and song birds, around 80 percent of the whole white stork population, as well as two types of wild storks. Most of the resting places are located along the northern Black Sea coast, near Kaliakra and Balchik, around the lakes by Durankulak and Schabla, as well as at Cape Emine and Sozopol.

HORO

This round dance is an essential component of every village festival, but in addition it can be seen in tourist centres at taverns that offer a folklore programme. It is a dance which Bulgarians also perform in the major towns and cities at weddings and other major celebrations, and more and more young people are taking it up.

Don't let yourself be put off by the complicated and frequent changes of beat. Just join in! The leading dancers are very flexible and frequently improvise the different steps. When you first join the circle you may miss the beat now and again, but you won't ever be allowed to drop out of the dance because your neighbours will happily hold you tight and patiently get you back into the rhythm.

MARTENITSA

On 1 March people throughout the country present one another with a martenitsa – red and white woollen tassels, usually two, which are knotted together at the top and dangle from a red

is coniferous forest, especially on the Pirin and Rila Mountains, much of the remainder being deciduous forest. Only occasionally will you come across wild animals, but in the wooded mountain regions there are brown bears, wolves, lynx, foxes, wild boar, deer, roe and chamois. The wild animals and their habitats are, however, under threat from the construction of new hotel and residential complexes in the vicinity of the National Park and nature reserves, for example on the Black Sea Coast and in the Pirin Mountains. People keep buffalos, donkeys and mules as pets.

Water pollution and over-fishing have

and white braided thread. By offering the martenitsa you are wishing the recipient good health and at the same time celebrating the advent of spring. It's worn on clothing or around the wrist or neck, until the wearer sees a stork or swallow returning from migration; it is then removed and hung on a tree in blossom. Traditionally the martenitsa was also considered a symbol of fertility, which is why it is sometimes hung on young animals.

MEDICAL TOURISM

Eastern Europe is becoming an increasingly popular destination for medical tourists and Bulgaria is part of this business. Dental practices and specialist clinics compete to offer their services with well-trained specialist staff and low prices. There are several dental clinics in Varna and on the Black Sea, and travel agencies will make arrangements for the tourists' stay. This sounds very attractive, but there's always the risk that treatment on the cheap doesn't work.

MINORITIES

More than a sixth of Bulgaria's total population of approx. 7.5 million inhabitants are not South Slavs, but belong to one of the national or ethnic and religious minorities: 800,000 Turks, 250,000 to 300,000 Bulgarian-speaking Muslims (who do not like to be referred to as 'Pomaks') and at least 400,000 Roma.

The relationship between Bulgarians and Turks deteriorated rapidly in the middle of the 1980s when, in 1984, the Communist Party launched a 'Bulgarianisation' campaign and forced the Turks to take Bulgarian names and to abandon their customs and even the use of their own language in public. In a mass exodus in 1989, around 300,000 Turks left the country,

just over half of them returning after the end of the one-party state. Since the beginning of the 1990s Bulgarian-Turkish relations have stabilised, which was helped by giving the Turkish minority political representation.

But a much more serious issue in the recent past has been the problematical situation of the Roma who are distributed all over the country and live in ghetto-like areas on the outskirts of the major towns and cities. The Roma are rejected by all other ethnic groups and even those Roma willing to seek integration meet with unanimous rejection. In some smaller towns this has led to parts of the Roma districts becoming no-go areas for non-Roma.

Dzhumaja Mosque in Plovdiv

In parade uniform – changing the guard at the Presidential Palace

MUSIC

The Bulgarians are a music-loving people; they enjoy making music and adore their musicians. Music plays a major role in marriage ceremonies and the call-up for military service, traditionally the most important occasions and ones which have almost become ritual festivities. Young Bulgarians also love chalga, a form of folk music, strongly influence by pop and characterised by repeated musical themes and dance rhythms. With the collapse of the Communist regime, restrictions on broadcasting such music were lifted and a new generation of musicians adopted *chalga,* grabbing the public spotlight by performing daring and overtly sexual songs not previously allowed. Nowadays pop folk concerts with the stars and starlets of this type of music are held in the summer all over the country. Many major towns and cities have developed their own techno scene separate from mainstream. Have a listen, for example, to Miss Lidiya, known as Bulgaria's 'First Lady Of Techno' who is said to be one of the most promising and attractive newcomers on the Bulgarian electronic music scene.

NATIONAL REVIVAL

The period between 1762 and 1878 is recorded in the country's history books as the time of the National Revival which sowed the seeds for the cultural, spiritual and political life of modern Bulgaria. The monk Paisij, who in 1762 completed the first work about Slav and Bulgarian history, provided the initial impetus for this cultural awakening, the first phase of the Revival. The main aim of his work was to awaken in the people a national awareness of their past, language and customs. In the 19th century the movement launched by Paisij led to the struggle for schools of their own, an independent church and severance from the Greek Patriarchate in Constantinople, which was achieved in 1870. By this time a partly national, partly democratic movement had developed which took up the struggle for political and state liberation from the Ottoman Empire. The climax of this movement was the April Uprising in 1876 which was brutally put down.

One of the victims of this uprising was Christo Botev, the Bulgarian national poet and freedom fighter. Two years after his death, as a consequence of the Russo-Turkish War, Bulgaria finally achieved its national independence. The story of the April Uprising, an event which cost many revolutionaries their lives, has become a heroic legend and is now embedded in the nation's collective memory. At the stroke of midday on 2 June, the anniversary of Christo Botev's death, sirens throughout the country are sounded, people stop work and traffic comes to a standstill in memory of the poet and the aims of his generation.

POLITICS

The end of the Communist era was marked by free elections in 1990. Bulgaria has been a republic since 1991, its political system being a parliamentary democracy. The country joined Nato in 2004 and became a member of the EU in 2007. But the foundations of the constitutional state are still rather unstable as Bulgaria struggles with corruption and organised crime. The embezzlement of EU finance in 2008 even led to Brussels putting a cap on financial aid to the country.

The ruling party is the GERB, the 'Citizens for European Development'. The current Prime Minister Boyko Borisov owes his electoral success not only to his clear populist appeal, but also to his declaration of war on organised crime and corruption. Lots of Bulgarians are sceptical as to whether he will achieve his aims. Nonetheless – not least because of pressure from Brussels – a specialist court has been established and a state prosecutor with the powers to challenge organised crime appointed. The customs service has also been restructured.

RAKIA

For many Bulgarians, brandy is not a drink for the end of a meal, but rather something to enjoy as an aperitif, because a genuine Bulgarian meal usually begins with a small salad and a *rakia*. The Bulgarian national drink is a high-proof fruit brandy, usually distilled from plums or grapes. The best of these brandies are to be enjoyed, of course, with locals in their homes. Distilling brandy is not only legal in Bulgaria, it's virtually a national pastime. And it goes without saying that

lots of Bulgarians compete to distil the best home-produced brandy. Most of them are tasty, pure and palatable – if you don't try to match the customary measures preferred by some locals.

SAINTS DAYS

The Bulgarians hardly acknowledge their birthdays, but they celebrate all the more intensely their relevant saint's day. People call in uninvited on the person whose saint's day it is and pay their respects. Popular saints days are, for example, 1 January – Vassil, 6 May – Georgi, 6 December – Nikolai and 27 December – Stefan. Ancient Bulgarian customs are celebrated on the most important saints days throughout the country: lamb is eaten on St George's Day; horse races are held on St Todor's Day; and young men leap into the cold rivers on St Jordan's Day to retrieve a cross from the water.

YOGHURT

The Bulgarian natural yoghurt *kiselo mljako* (sour milk) really can work miracles – well, at least that's what the Bulgarians say. It ensures a long, healthy life, improves the skin, soothes sun burn and helps digestion. The Bulgarians eat yoghurt at every meal, prepared as a starter and dessert, as a side dish to the main course or for breakfast. It's also eaten as a snack between meals.

Bulgarian yoghurt is produced mainly from cow's milk with the help of the unique bacterial culture Lactobacillus bulgaricus. Yoghurt made from sheep or buffalo milk is also considered a particular speciality. These types have a higher fat content and stronger taste. The more fat that yoghurt contains, the firmer is its consistency. If you ask a Bulgarian, then the best yoghurt is always the one you can cut with a knife.

FOOD & DRINK

Food is an important business for the Bulgarians and a typical meal is tasty and varied, with some unmistakable Turkish influences.

The quality and choice of restaurants is now better than ever. In addition to classic restaurants, there are small, traditionally furnished inns *(han, hanche)*. *Mehana* is what people used to call the simple tavern, and today these typically Bulgarian bars, with traditional decoration and music, serve fresh salads, food from the grill and regional dishes, as well as beer, brandy and wine, of course. In recent years lots of cafés with a modern decor have opened, offering a wide range of starters, main courses and desserts both at midday and in the evening. And you'll also find pizzerias and international fast food restaurants in the larger towns and cities and in the tourist centres.

Although there is now a wide range of so-called coffee houses, the traditional *sladkarnica* has retained its popularity. The 'place for sweetness' (a literal translation) is a mixture of patisserie and traditional café, frequented by locals. When ordering a coffee remember to say what sort you want (espresso, cappuccino, instant or Turkish coffee) and, to be on the safe side, how sweet you want it since, for example, Turkish coffee is made with the sugar already added. In addition there are loads of booths and stalls and, since the Bulgarians love to nibble, you'll see people selling peanuts, sunflower and pumpkin seeds everywhere.

Photo: Gyuvech, a Bulgarian speciality baked in a pot

Mountains of water melons and a brandy as an aperitif – here's an introduction to Bulgarian cuisine

Prices in restaurants are perfectly reasonable, a meal for two with a bottle of Bulgarian wine seldom costing more than 60 leva. Only in the large tourist centres do prices begin to match what you'd expect to pay in western Europe.

Bulgarian cuisine is well-known for its liberal use of fruit and vegetables. Vast piles of water melons are stacked up by the roadsides from early summer onwards, replaced in the autumn by pumpkins and later by cabbages. People here are proud of their home-grown fruit and

it will become clear why when you taste your first Bulgarian tomato, if not before. Bulgaria is and remains a country where no genetically modified food is grown, the reason being the strict regulations protecting the nature reserves, areas of organic cultivation and beehives. Bulgaria is a land of amateur beekeepers and, with the number of beekeepers preferring organic farming having risen by 40% in recent years, there's hardly any room left for genetically modified crops. Areas planted with organic crops

LOCAL SPECIALITIES

▶ **Baklava** – very sweet filo pastry with syrup and usually filled with nuts
▶ **Banica** – filo pastry filled with ewe's cheese
▶ **Gyuvech** – a hot pot with a mixture of meat, vegetable and potatoes
▶ **Kachamak** – a sort of cornmeal porridge, topped with egg and cheese, served in an earthenware pot
▶ **Kavarma** – goulash of mutton or pork with vegetables and tomato purée, served in an earthenware pot
▶ **Kebapcheta** – small grilled rolls of minced meat
▶ **Kjopolu** – aubergine salad; it's not to be found everywhere, but when you come across it, you really must try it
▶ **Kyufte** – grilled minced meat balls
▶ **Lukanka** – salami-like sausage, cut into slices and served on platters
▶ **Meshana skara** – mixed grill
▶ **Musaka** – casserole with aubergines, tomatoes and chopped meat
▶ **Ovcharska** – shepherd's salad: mixed salad with ham, olives and grated ewe's cheese
▶ **Palachinka** – filled pancake (with chocolate, jam etc.)
▶ **Shopska salad** – the Bulgarian classic: tomato and cucumber salad with paprika and grated ewe's cheese on top (photo right)
▶ **Sirene po shopski** – ewe's cheese baked in an earthenware pot with tomatoes and egg
▶ **Skumria** – grilled mackerel, a classic Bulgarian dish
▶ **Snezhanka** – (Snow White) cucumber salad in thickened yoghurt, garnished with walnuts
▶ **Tarator** – cold cucumber soup, prepared with dill, walnuts and masses of garlic. Very refreshing, especially in the summer months (photo left)

in Bulgaria have increased approximately ten-fold since 2008, and the plan is now to extend organic farming so that in future 8 percent of agricultural land will be used for this purpose.

Breakfast in Bulgaria – as in all the southern European countries – has no great significance and it's often no more than a coffee and a cigarette for most Bulgarians. However, the vast majority of hotels have broadly adapted to northern European habits and now provide a wider range of dishes. But if you set off on your own in search of a breakfast, you'll probably need to try out the popular pastries, including *banica*, often known by its Turkish name of *bjurek*, which is a filo pastry usually filled with ewe's cheese, sometimes also with minced meat. It is available from local shops that combine a patisserie with a snack bar. The pancake-like *mekitsa* is made of kneaded dough and yoghurt; it is deep fried and then sweetened with icing sugar or honey and usually served with jam or sirene (white cheese) – children love it.

To accompany a brandy aperitif, the main meal of the day in Bulgaria, usually begins with a salad. There are endless varieties of fruit brandies, but the Bulgarians value *Troyanska Slivova*, a plum brandy, very highly. Also recommended are the somewhat milder *Muskatova* types, especially *Burgaska Muskatova* (plum) or *Slivenska Perla* (grape). Main courses are normally served with bread but no accompanying vegetables, so subject to your appetite, you may wish to order them separately.

Even the most basic restaurants serve a wide range of starters such as *kyopolou* (eggplants and garlic), liver or breaded ewe's cheese. Main meals are usually based on meat, and *kebapcheta* (minced beef and pork) and grilled steaks are very popular. Peppers or vine leaves stuffed with minced meat, with a vegetarian option also available, are typical. There are only two traditional types of Bulgarian cheese, sirene and kashkaval (hard yellow cheese), but it's remarkable how many different uses they're put to.

Desserts are usually very sweet and include various sorts of *baklava*, a filo pastry filled with chopped walnuts, sweetened with syrup or honey and spiced with cinnamon. Yoghurt with honey, crème caramel and ice cream are other typical desserts, as well as fresh fruit, depending on the season.

Wine waiter showcasing two fine vintages

Bulgarian wine can look back on a tradition of almost 5000 years. In his 'Iliad' Homer refers to the regular deliveries of Thracian wine reaching Troy and in the 'Odyssey' there's also mention of 'wine as sweet as honey'. It has to be said that the country is still no paradise for lovers of dry wine, but the range is becoming wider.

The best red wines are full-bodied and robust and many of the good white wines have a pleasant bouquet. Of the local grape varieties, based both on their quality and also their alcohol by volume, the best sellers are *Gamza, Mavrud, Pamid, Dimjat* and *Misket*. Mavrud from Asenovgrad and Misket Slavjanska are dessert wines.

SHOPPING

In Bulgaria it's shopping with a difference. If you're open to surprises, take your time to browse, soak up the atmosphere and don't regard the shopping trip as an extended walk. Basically, lots of traders sell everything they can get their hands on. And whether it's food, clothes or souvenirs, you'll always find that prices are significantly lower away from the tourist centres.

ART & ANTIQUES

The number of art galleries in the towns and tourist centres has risen enormously in recent years, and they sell all kinds of handicrafts – from paintings, sculptures and icons to jewellery and traditional costumes. You'll find furniture, clocks and watches, crockery and all sorts of bits and pieces in the antique shops which are mainly located in the larger towns and cities. They're often very small and crammed full but it's worthwhile taking your time and rummaging around. The prices are almost always negotiable.

BAZAARS

Try not to leave Bulgaria without having visited all the different types of market, and especially the bazaars where you'll gain a real insight into Bulgarian everyday life. Outside the towns and city centres, bazaars have been set up for which the term 'flea market' would be a compliment. All sorts of junk is offered for sale here, from rusty pitch forks to crackling gramophones. Many of the vendors come from Russia, China, Turkey and the former Yugoslavia and most dealers have fixed prices but are prepared to haggle. The *Stock Basaar Ilianci* in Sofia is the largest bazaar not only in Bulgaria, but in the whole of the Balkans.

CLOTHES & SHOES

There is a huge number of small boutiques in the towns and cities, and prices range from low to really expensive. Do be careful when buying items which purport to be branded goods because they're often just cheap imitations. Sofia is the best place to go shopping, with lots of international labels having outlets in the capital, and the prices are similar to those in western Europe. You can also find expensive local fashions, furs and luxury articles.

Bustling markets, small boutiques or large malls – you will be surprised at Bulgaria's offering

MARKETS

All the major towns and cities have at least one outdoor fruit and vegetable market. Farmers come in from the surrounding areas and sell their produce such as cheese, meat and eggs. The market is the centre of social life in the town, where people meet friends and acquaintances, drink coffee, philosophise about politics and discuss everyday matters. The women's market *(Zhenski Pazar)* in Sofia is very well-known and it's one of the few places in the city where you can still get a sense of how life used to be in the Balkans.

SHOPPING MALLS

The huge shopping centres, the malls, have also arrived in Bulgaria – and are booming. Not only can you shop there, but it is also the place to show off your new gear, meet your friends, have a bite to eat, go to the cinema and relax. There are malls with wi-fi in Sofia and Varna.

SOUVENIRS

Pottery, bone china tableware, leather goods, embroidery (blouses, table-cloths) and copper and pewter vessels are always good souvenirs. You'll often come across women in the street selling crocheted or lace table-cloths, scarves and shawls. Other typical souvenirs include rose oil (in small, pretty, wooden containers), dolls in traditional costume and woodcarvings. The shops run by the Association of Bulgarian Artists offer sophisticated items of this sort, as well as other types of souvenir.

SPIRITS

It's worth taking a bottle of *Trojanska Slivova*, the plum brandy, back home, as well as *Pliska* brandy, *Mastika* anise brandy or the best red wines. But it's wise to be careful if you're offered imported drinks at incredibly low prices from stalls by the roadside: they don't always contain what the label suggests.

THE PERFECT ROUTE

BIG CITY AMBIENCE IN BULGARIA'S CAPITAL

The capital **①** *Sofia* → **p. 44** is the starting point for a perfect day's trip through Bulgaria. Culture and nightlife, history and modernity – Sofia has it all (photo left). And do make sure you allow yourself time for a stop in one of the countless street cafés, so you can strike up a conversation with the locals. The Sofians meet up at all times of the day over an espresso. They are friendly and happy to talk.

MOUNTAINS AND A WORLD-FAMOUS MONASTERY

Highway no. 1 heading south goes past the Vitosha Mountains through the narrow Vladaja Gorge. As soon as you turn off towards **②** **Rila Monastery** → **p. 41**, if not before, you'll find yourself in another world: the air is crisp, the mountain backdrop impressive, the villages simple. This world-famous monastery is the starting point for tours in the Rila Mountains. Then return to Highway no. 1 and continue along the River Struma, a paradise for anglers and white-water enthusiasts, until Highway no. 19 turns off to the east through the Rila and Pirin Mountains to **③** **Bansko** → **p. 35**. This city is not only the starting point for mountain hikes and a popular winter sport centre, but is also well-known for its many taverns serving excellent Bulgarian food.

ON THE WAY TO THE UNDERWORLD

The route then heads eastwards through the Rhodopes. According to legend, Orpheus descended via a cave in the gorge **④** *Trigradsko Zhdrelo* → **p. 64** into the underworld as he searched for his beloved wife. You'll come across tobacco farmers, bagpipe players and cave climbers in the Rhodopes. Take the road to Pamporovo and then Highway no. 86 heading north past **⑤** **Bachkovo Monastery** → **p. 62** (photo right). The ruined castle **⑥** **Asenova Krepost** → **p. 62** towers up over the road and then from here cast a final look back towards the Rhodopes.

BULGARIA WITH ALL ITS TRADITIONS

Not far to the north you come to **⑦** **Plovdiv** → **p. 56**. Stroll through the narrow streets of Bulgaria's finest Old Town and enjoy a typical

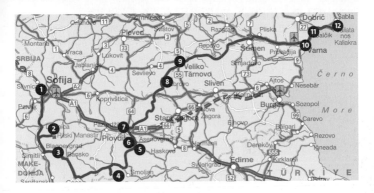

Latin atmosphere. Thracians, Romans, Ottomans and Bulgars have all left their traces in the architecture. From here Highway no. 56 runs through Rose Valley to the Shipka Pass. Situated to the north of the pass are the fascinating museum villages of ⑧ Et-ara and Bozhentsi → p. 70, with their traditional houses and artisans' streets, and here you can admire the old arts and crafts as well as take part in a handicraft course.

OLD CAPITAL AND BATHING BEACHES

The road to the Black Sea coast goes via the old capital city of ⑨ *Veliko Tarnovo* → p. 66 which is a must-see for all those with an interest in history and church fres-coes. The houses hang from the steep cliffs like swallows' nests. In the Black Sea city of ⑩ Varna → p. 85 the beach is only a stone's throw from the city centre, so a pair of swimming trunks or a bikini might come in useful. The atmosphere in the city is easy-going, the climate mild and in the summer there's a gentle, cooling breeze.

WILD COAST AND GENTLE BEACHES

The further north follow Highway no. 9, the bleaker the landscape becomes. Be-tween Varna and ⑪ *Balchik* → p. 92 there are countless beaches, and the steep coast at ⑫ Cape Kaliakra and Ka-men Bryag → p. 93 is very impressive with its high cliffs and rare flora and fauna. The stretch between Kamen Bry-ag and Tyulenovo (8km/5mi) is ideally suited for a walking tour and with a little bit of luck you'll be able to watch dol-phins at play.

975 km (600 mi). Driving time: 17 hours.
Recommended length of trip: one week
Detailed map of the route on
the back cover, in the road atlas
and the pull-out map

WESTERN BULGARIA

Western Bulgaria basically consists of three parts ... and they could not be more different.

The northwest of the country – still pretty much untouched by tourism – is thinly populated, has a weak economy and the state of some roads leaves a lot to be desired.

The southwest, on the other hand, shaped by the primeval forces of nature, is much easier for holidaymakers to travel around. The high peaks of the Rila and Pirin Mountains dominate the landscape, and in this region you'll find the most attractive ski resorts and walking areas.

The metropolis of Sofia is surrounded by mountains. It's by far and away the largest city in the country, with one in five Bulgarians living there. The city's significance is based on its location at the crossroads of the main lines of communication in the Balkans, with routes from Vienna to Istanbul, from the Black Sea to the Adriatic and from the Danube to the Aegean passing through. The strategic location attracted early settlers and later generals and conquerors. After the fragmentation of the Ottoman Empire in 1878, the city was named as the capital of a Bulgarian state for the first time, and this began its rapid expansion which saw it grow from a city of about 20,000 inhabitants to a metropolis with a million in less than a century. It was at this time that they coined the phrase, which Sofia is happy to proclaim as its motto: 'Ever growing, never ageing'.

The city's scenic location is one of its main attractions. It is bordered to the

Photo: Sofia, in the foreground the Baths Mosque

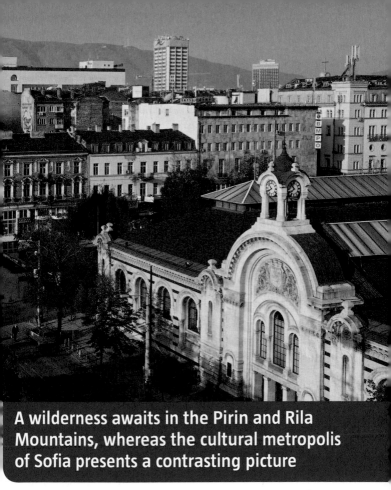

A wilderness awaits in the Pirin and Rila Mountains, whereas the cultural metropolis of Sofia presents a contrasting picture

north by the Balkans, to the east by the Sredna Gora Mountains and to the south, less than an hour's drive away, by the Rila Mountains. But the icing on the cake is the Vitosha Massif, a range to the southwest on the immediate outskirts of the city. Less than 10km/6mi from the centre, the foothills rise up over the city – as its ever present companion, visible from far and wide. So it goes without saying that the Vitosha Massif has always been a very popular spot for a day out for the Sofians.

If you'd prefer to spend part of your holiday away from the hustle and bustle of the usual tourist destinations and get a flavour of the real Bulgaria, then you'll be amply rewarded by a stay in the southwest of the country. With its two mountain ranges, numerous lakes, rivers and mineral springs, picturesque villages and old monasteries, the area offers a scenic and cultural diversity which is almost unique for being so unspoilt. The dominant features are the Pirin and Rila Mountains, the Pirin with a somewhat wilder appearance

The Rila Mountains reward walkers with a view of lakes dating from the Ice Age

although it is easily accessible. Because of the wealth and diversity of the flora and fauna, an area of 170sq.mi in the Pirin Mountains has been given the status of a Unesco-protected **INSIDER TIP** **National Park**. Mountain walking trails lead to the peaks of the Vichren (2914m/9560ft), Kutelo (2908m/9541ft) and Todorka (2746m/9010ft), past many of the glaciers which total almost 180.

The Rila Mountains also offer impressive sights with their 132 peaks over 2000 metres (6526 feet), of which 78 attain a height of more than 2500m/8203ft, including the Musala, at 2925m/9597ft the highest mountain peak in southeast Europe. Lying between the steep mountain peaks in clearly defined glacial valleys are the 'eyes' of the mountain range: 140 lakes dating from the Ice Age. A particularly stunning sight is the view of the **INSIDER TIP** **seven Rila lakes** at an altitude of 2200m/7218ft to 2500m/8203ft. The Rila Mountains are also the source of the country's longest

rivers – with the exception of the Danube – the Iskar, Maritsa and Mesta, as well as countless mineral springs. This is why there's a concentration of spas and health resorts (Sandanski, Velingrad, Devin, Kyustendil) in the southwest.

The monasteries represent the best way of finding a point of contact with Bulgaria's past and first and foremost you should visit Rilski manastir (Rila Monastery), not only a national shrine but a World Heritage Site. Then there's Rozhen Monastery, situated not far from Melnik, where you can admire the beautifully crafted woodcarvings. But a stroll through the villages also recalls Macedonia's eventful history and perhaps at times its present because, with the Pirin area, the southwest comprises that region of Macedonia which became part of Bulgaria in the partition of 1913. Numerous monuments, museums and town names are dedicated to protagonists of the Macedonian movement, such as Goce Delchev and Jane Sandansky.

BANSKO

(131 D4) *(𝓜 C7)* ★ ☼ **The town of Bansko (pop. 12,000), lying in Razlog Valley at the foot of the Pirin Mountains, is the entrance to the Pirin National Park.**

In recent years this area, characterised by long winters with lots of snow and short, cool summers, has developed into the country's leading winter sports centre. Almost overnight this small romantic town has grown into an international winter sports centre, though it has to be said that Bulgarian environmentalists view the development with some concern. The rapid increase in ski tourism is destroying the environment, forests hundreds of years old are giving way to countless new ski runs and hotels.

When there's no snow, it's essentially the old town centre which attracts tourists. Labyrinthine alleys, cobbled streets and typical Bulgarian half-timbered houses with their inner courtyards typify the old, original Bansko. It's easy to get lost but there's always Mount Todorka towering over the city to help you get your bearings. Women sell handmade tablecloths, socks and caps, and on bank holidays the locals get their national costumes out of the wardrobe.

As early as the 18th century Bansko had developed into a thriving religious centre, thanks not only to trade and arts and craft, but also to its advantageous position on the connecting route between the Aegean and central Europe. Evidence for this is everywhere in the numerous Revival houses in the town. The town holds a jazz festival every year in August, with visitors and performers coming from all over the world to listen to the music in all its many guises, and especially in the evenings the town is transformed into a grand popular festival. Today there's a lot of building work going on in the town, with local and foreign investors erecting large complexes, hotels and holiday flats on the outskirts. Situated only 160km/100mi from the capital, Bansko is today a popular holiday destination for Sofians. Lots of visitors also come from Greece, a close neighbour, and the town has been quick to adapt, with the number of hotels in-

MARCO POLO HIGHLIGHTS

★ Bansko
The small town has become an international winter sports destination almost overnight → p. 35

★ Rilski manastir
Rila Monastery symbolises the significance of the Orthodox Church in Bulgaria's history → p. 41

★ Melnik
Bulgaria's smallest town lies amongst vineyards and ruins → p. 42

★ Sveti Aleksandar Nevski Cathedral
Regarded as the symbol of Sofia, this historic church is considered by many to be the finest 20th-century building in the Balkans → p. 48

★ Boyanskata Tsarkva
Bulgarian paintings from the Middle Ages adorn this church – in a beautiful setting → p. 52

★ Vitosha Mountains
A walk to the Golden Bridges or a walk to the Black Peak → p. 53

creasing several fold. Nowhere else in western Bulgaria will you find so many mehanas so close together. These small taverns offer traditional, regional dishes, most of them with lots of meat, and local musicians often lay on the entertainment. *www.bansko24.com, www.bansko.bg*

SIGHTSEEING

BANSKO OLD TOWN

The houses in the old town date from its heyday in the 18th and 19th century. They have two faces and are reminiscent of monastery architecture in that to the street outside they present a severe, al-most off-putting stone facade. A typical feature is the closed wooden balcony called a *chardak*. In olden times the hole in the middle was meant to hold a musket, in case enemies or criminals stopped outside in the street. Unfortunately, advertising hoardings now conceal the facades of the old houses.

The inner courtyards with their carved banisters and columns create a warm, welcoming impression. Woodwork is a characteristic of the interiors and in the Revival period the masters of the Bansko school of woodcarvers were considered the best in the whole region. The *Sirleshtov House (Ulitsa Jane Sandanski 12)* is the oldest preserved house in Bansko, with a hiding place in the cellar. The *Veljanov House (Ulitsa Veljan Ognev 5)* has a well-preserved interior decoration and murals. In the *Neofit Rilski House (Ulitsa Pirin 17)* there is a still functioning bread oven and a traditional classroom.

SVETA TROITSA (CHURCH OF THE HOLY TRINITY) ●

The church was built in 1835 by local craftsmen, and in the courtyard there stands a 30-m high bell and clock tower. The church has its own choir and there are services twice a day. On Saturdays, Sundays and on religious holidays the seven church bells in the tower are rung by hand, with the bell ringers playing a tune unique to Bansko which has been handed down from generation to generation. *Ploshtad Vazrazhdane | tel. 0749 8 83 44*

FOOD & DRINK

BARYAKOVA MEHANA

Baryakova Mehana is situated in the centre of the old town, not far from the church, on the ground floor of a house dating from the 19th century. The dining area is the family's former living room,

LOW BUDGET

▶ Culture at a knock-down price: classical music, opera and theatre in Sofia for 10 to 30 leva. Concerts are held in the Bulgarian Hall *(Zala Balgarija | Ulitsa Aksakov 1 | tel. 02 9 87 76 56)*. The ● *National Opera (Ulitsa Vrabcha 1 | tel. 02 9 87 13 66 | www.operasofia. bg)* has produced some world stars and here you can listen to the talented new generation of singers. In the Ivan Vazov National Theatre *(Ulitsa Djakon Ignatij 5 | tel. 02 8 11 92 27 | www.nationaltheatre.bg)* the classics of literature are performed.

▶ Reasonable accommodation is available in the Rila and Pirin Mountains at mountain huts, in shared rooms. Sleeping bag, walking maps, suitable clothing and boots are important. Information at the *Bulgarian Tourist Board BTS (Sofia | Bulevard Vasil Levski 75 | tel. 02 9 80 12 85 | www. btsbg.org)*.

with the family now living on the second floor. In the summer there is service in the inner courtyard. The mehana offers original specialities such as INSIDER TIP stuffed pork and homemade bread. It's best to reserve a table, especially at weekends. *Ulitsa Veljan Ognev 31 | tel. 0749 8 44 48 40 | Moderate*

In recent years Bansko has become the number one destination for winter sports in Bulgaria. It has also made a name for itself internationally and it's here that races for the Alpine Skiing World Cup are held. The ski resort com-

The interior and the murals in the Veljanov House are well preserved

VODENITSATA MEHANA
Vodenitsata (Watermill) Mehana offers traditional food in a convivial, authentic atmosphere. In the winter, meals are grilled on the open fire in the dining room and there are local dishes such as *kapama* (various types of meat with stewed cabbage and rice) and *chumlek* (beef and potato casserole). At weekends the ● *Banski Starcheta* (Bansko altos) appear, singing Bansko songs and playing traditional instruments such as the bagpipes and clarinet, and locals dance to the music. *Ulitsa Vasil Levski 1 | tel. 0888 55 11 10 | Moderate*

prises more than 75km/47mi of ski runs at all degrees of difficulty and 27km/17mi of ski lifts which ensure that skiers can access altitudes between 1000m/3280ft and 2600m/8530ft. The lower gondola station is located in Pirin Street when leaving the old town and from here you can get up to Mount Todorka. The ski season lasts from December to May *(www.banskoski.com)*. There are several ski schools in the town, as well as a freerider school. Ask for Maya in the *Ski Rental Shop* in the *Royal Towers Hotel (Ulitsa Yavor 1 | tel. 0887 56 76 72 | www.oxo.bg)*.

BANSKO

WHERE TO STAY

HOTEL BISSER

This friendly family hotel has a free sauna and lounge with an open fireplace; it offers views of the Pirin Mountains, but there's no car park. Lunch and evening meal are available on request to guests and the food is home-made. To accompany the meal, the landlord Georgi Obecanov will entertain with amusing stories. *20 rooms | Ulitsa El-Tepe 16 | tel. 0749 8 28 17 | www.bisser-bansko.com | Budget*

KEMPINSKI HOTEL GRAND ARENA

This hotel comprising several buildings is situated near the gondola station. The rooms are spacious and elegantly furnished. In the hotel there's a spa and fitness area with various saunas and swimming pools and there's also a snow room to cool off at minus 15°C/5°F. *159 rooms | Ulitsa Pirin 96 | tel. 0749 88 88 88 | www.kempinski.com/en/bansko | Expensive*

BIOHOTEL MORAVSKO VILLAGE ⟳

This new family hotel is approx. 10km/6mi outside Bansko near the Predela Pass, just off the main road. The complex consists of four two-storey buildings with a garden. The hotel's own restaurant serves dishes made from genuinely organic food, in part home-produced. *16 rooms | signposted at the Predela Pass | tel. 0898 62 17 65 | www.biohotel-bg.com | Budget*

HOTEL RODINA

With a central location on the main shopping street and now re-opened after renovations (all 35 double rooms are now en suite), the hotel offers typical Bulgarian furnishings and decor, with sauna *and a mehana* serving local specialities. *41 rooms | I Ulitsa Pirin 7 I | tel. 0749 8 81 06 | hoteli.bansko.net | Moderate*

INFORMATION

Ploshtad Nikola Vaptsarov 1 (in the town hall) | tel. 0749 8 85 80 | infocenter@bansko.bg

WHERE TO GO

DOBARSKO (131 D4) (*ฬ C7*)

Dobarsko, 20km/12mi from Bansko, is situated between the Pirin and Rila Mountains. On the walls of the St Theodore Tyro and St Theodore Stratelates church there's a painting showing INSIDER TIP *Jesus taking off in a space ship*. Why? Well, that's something locals and even experts have been wondering about for decades. The church was built in the 17th century and its murals are amongst the best in Bulgaria. It's now a museum which is open to visitors every day. Should the door be shut, ask for the mayor, who has the key.

The small village is a wonderful starting point for lots of mountain hikes in the southern Rila Mountains, and it also offers water sports such as rowing and motorboats. The village also boasts a huge waterfall – the Shtrokaloto – which falls from a height of 24 metres. *(www.bansko.org/dobarsko)*.

MINERAL BATHS

You'll find therapeutic baths and climatotherapy centres in many localities in the southwest, the largest being *Sandanski* **(130 C5)** (*ฬ C8*), the regional centre for spa treatments. The *Interhotel Sandanski* is allegedly the largest balneology centre for the treatment of bronchial asthma *(East of the town | 296 rooms | tel. 0746 3 11 65 | www.ihsand.com | Moderate–Expensive)*. The ● *Hotel Medite SPA Resort* in Sandanski *(prop. Ulitsa Polenishki | tel. 0746 3 32 00 | www.hotelmedite.com | Moderate–Expensive)* provides treatments carried out using mineral water and there are even pools filled with mineral water. In *Velingrad* (131 E3) *(ꕷ D7)* they specialise in phytotherapy (treatments using natural plant extracts) and in *Kyustendil* (130 A–B2) *(ꕷ A6)* guests love the mud baths.

PARK ZA TANZUVASHTI MECHKI (BELITSA DANCING BEARS PARK)
(131 D4) *(ꕷ D5)*

Here, on a 30-acre site, 24 bears which had previously been kept as dancing bears have been given a new home with

PIRIN NATIONAL PARK
(130–131 C–D 4–5) *(ꕷ C7–8)*

The Unesco-listed Pirin National Park is situated south of Bansko. About 80 per-cent of its surface area of 10,000 acres is covered with forest. In the National Park you'll find 176 mountain lakes as well as Mount Vichren, the highest peak in the Pirin Mountains at 2914m/9560ft.

The landscape itself is magnificent. The best time for INSIDER TIP mountain hikes in the National Park and in the Pirin Mountains as a whole extends from the

Large brown resident in the Belitsa Bear Park, a retirement home for ex-dancing bears

forest, caves and ponds. This, the largest bear sanctuary in Europe, is situated some 30km/20mi north of Bansko and 12km/8mi north of the town of Belitsa in the Rila Mountains; however, it has to be said that the road between Belitsa and the bear park is in very poor condition. *www.vier-pfoten.bg | daily from 10am, closing time season dependent, guided tours every hour April–Nov.*

beginning of July to the middle of September, and the walking trails have both summer and winter markings. Above the tree line the land is stony and has an alpine character. Mountain huts provide board and lodging, but it has to be said that the ones you find in Bulgaria are very basic. Bansko is a good starting point for walks, with many of the hotels there organising mountain tours. From Bansko either walk or take the lift to the *Vihren mountain hut* (four hours) and then proceed to the ❅ *Vihren peak* (seven hours there and back). To get to the *Demyanitsa hut* take the lift to the *Shiligarnika area*.

A popular walking trail, part of which you can also do by lift if you want, runs from Dobrinishte to the *Bezbog hut*, then via the *Tevno Ezero* refuge to the *Demjanitsa hut* and back to Bansko. Note that walking in the high mountains is challenging and only possible with overnight stops. Camping and fishing are not allowed in the National Park.

INSIDER TIP ▶ RIBARNIKA (FISH LAKE) (131 D4) *(𝄞 C6)*

You can enjoy the best grilled fish in the *Ribarnika* complex, 4km/2.5mi from Dobrinishte (direction *Goce-Delchev mountain hut*), and you can catch your own trout too.

RILA WALKS ● (130–131 C–D3) *(𝄞 C6)*

The finest, and also very popular, walking destinations in the Rila Mountains are: ❅ *Musala Tour* (seven hours): the hike to the highest peak in southeast Europe (2925m/9597ft) starts from *Borovets*. Take the chair lift to the *Jastrebec summit* and then proceed via the *Musala mountain hut* to the summit, from which there's a magnificent view to enjoy. If you want to experience the summit early in the morning and get the clearest view, you should spend the night at a height of 2707m/8882ft in the *Everest refuge*, also known as the 'Ice Lake' *(Lednoto Ezero)*. From here it's only 30 minutes to the summit, but be aware a reservation is needed for a stay at the refuge *(tel. 0722 66 50 5, 0885 45 70 10)*.

Seven Rila Lakes: Take the bus from *Borovets* to the *Vada mountain hut* where you start the three-hour ascent to

Rila Monastery – national shrine and World Cultural Heritage Site

a fascinating group of mountain lakes. The *Sedemte Ezera* mountain h*ut* with 100 beds is situated in the vicinity of Fish Lake, the sixth lake. From here, you can continue with a six-hour hike over the beautiful *Partizanska Poljana mountain pasture* to the *Rila Monastery*. Borovets is a good starting point for a mountain hike (excellent bus connections to Sofia, lift in direction of Musala summit).

Tourist Information (in the hotels) organises walks. The largest office is in the *Hotel Samokov (306 rooms | tel. 0750 3 23 06 | www.samokov.com | Moderate–Expensive).*

RILSKI MANASTIR (RILA MONASTERY)

★ ● (130 C3) *(🕮 C6)*

In the forest at a height of 1147m/3763ft you suddenly come across a fortification wall 24m high in places. From the outside there's nothing to suggest that there is anything here, other than the remains of a castle. It almost seems as though the mighty wall wants to deny you access. But then, at the end of the only entry point to the south, you will stand entranced by the stunning beauty of the complex which exudes peace and harmony.

The monastery was founded in the 10th century by the hermit Ivan Rilski and bears testimony to the importance of the Orthodox Church in Bulgarian history. The oldest building is the *Chrelyo Tower*, erected in 1335 and named after its builder Dragovol Chrelyo. Everything else dates from the 19th century. The centrepiece and jewel in the crown of the art treasures is the main *Sveta Bogorodica* (Holy Mother of God) church, a combination of the old, triple-naved basilica, the cross-domed church on Mount Athos and the Italian domed church. The most celebrated masters of Bulgarian architecture, painting and woodcarving from the period of the National Revival worked on it. The outstanding features are the luminous frescoes in the interior and in the arcades, as well as the gold-plated iconostasis (altar wall) with 36 statues. The grave of Boris III, the last Bulgarian tsar, is also to be found in the main church.

Don't fail to have a look at the *Museum* with the original 14th-century door of the Chrelyo Tower, icons from the 14th and 15th century, the wooden cross made by the monk Rafail, which is a masterpiece of miniature carving (he worked on it for 12 years using magnifying glasses!), wall paintings from the 14th century located in the Chrelyo Tower itself and the original monastery kitchen dating from 1817 with all the utensils of that time. *The complex is open daily from dawn till dusk, but the museum facilities and the church close at 5pm. Museum entry: 8 lv | www.rilamonastery.pmg-blg.com*

The best place to stay the night is the monastery itself, though the monks think of it as a hostel for pilgrims and not as a hotel. Nevertheless, it might be worthwhile speaking to the monks, and you could also enquire in advance whether a reservation is possible *(tel. 0896 87 20 10)*. Immediately adjacent to the monastery, the *Rila Restaurant (Budget)* serves Bulgarian dishes. You can enjoy a lovely ☼ view from the terrace, though it's a bit small. They also offer reasonable, very simple rooms *(Budget)*. Other hotels are to be found on the road to the monastery or spend the night at the *Hotel Rilec (84 rooms | tel. 07054 21 06 | Budget)* approx. 2km/1mi further east.

MELNIK

(130 C5) (ⅅ C8) ★ **Now the smallest town in Bulgaria, in 1880 Melnik had 20,000 inhabitants, only 1000 fewer than Sofia had at that time. The Second Balkan War in 1913 almost completely destroyed the town and with it the trade routes.**

Today 250 people live here – earning a living mainly from wine, tobacco and tourism. Lying concealed amongst the sandstone pyramids, the town exudes a rather unreal atmosphere and it's not just because of the number of inhabitants – the ruins continually draw the visitor's attention to the town's decline. As though in an amphitheatre, unique monuments of relatively old and more recent architecture rise up amidst the steep flanks of the picturesque sandstone cliffs. They are home to really beautiful woodcarvings, icons, painted glass and murals. Paths, lined with grass and wormwood, snake through jagged cliffs and at their end you are met with a magical ☼ view; and while wandering around encounter again and again the vines which the area has to thank for the heavy, dark red wine.

Once there were more than 3600 houses with a fine architectural pedigree, but no more than 100 have been preserved, although these include quite a number of real gems. The extensive wine cellars are an object of particular fascination. They've been hollowed out beneath the cliffs and houses, so that a constant temperature can be guaranteed. Melnik manages to do without street names, but you won't have any difficulty finding the sights.

SIGHTSEEING

BOLJARSKATA KASHTA (BOYAR HOUSE)

The town's oldest house, dating from the 10th or 11th century, is unfortunately not in a good state of preservation. It once belonged to the Despot Slav.

GRADSKI MUZEJ (MUNICIPAL MUSEUM)

The museum in the Pashov House (Pashovata Kashta) dating from 1815 has wonderful wood-carved ceilings and marble fireplaces. *Daily 9am–midday and 1–5pm*

KORDOPULOVATA KASHTA (KORDOPULOV HOUSE)

This four-storey house dating from 1754 used to belong to a wine merchant. Particularly attractive are the 24 double rows of windows in the drawing room, the upper row made of Venetian coloured glass. The tour concludes with a wine tasting in the cellar hewn out of the cliffs. Here you'll find INSIDER TIP red wine maturing in huge casks, some of them holding 10,000 litres! *Daily 9am–8pm*

FOOD & DRINK

There are various wine cellars *(vinarna)* in the town, serving Melnik's most important product: red wine. Melnik's grape variety is one of the oldest in Bulgaria and grows exclusively in this region and around the neighbouring villages. It's typified by small berries and a thin, bluish-black skin. The wines which are then pressed from these grapes are heavy, have a characteristic aroma, a rich, dark red colour and a high alcohol content; they can be stored for several years in oak barrels. However, in recent years, Melnik wine has been subject to strong competition from other Bulgarian and imported wines.

MENCHEVA KASHTA

A typical Bulgarian *mehana* serving outstanding local food. *Near the Kordopulov House | tel. 07437 3 39 | Budget–Moderate*

WHERE TO STAY

LITOVA KASHTA

A comfortable hotel with three storeys. The speciality here is *meshaniza ot melnik* (mixture from Melnik) with meat and vegetables. Hotel staff organise outings by horse-drawn carriage or limo and there are also stables and ponies. *10 rooms, 2 apartments | tel. 07437 23 13 | litovakushta.com | Budget*

INFORMATION

MILUSHEVA KASHTA

Also gives advice on private accommodation in the town. *Near the post office | tel. 07437 3 26*

WHERE TO GO

ROZHENSKI ROZHEN (ROZHEN MONASTERY) (130 C5) (*∅ C8*)

This monastery is one of the oldest in Bulgaria. The complex 6km/4mi to the northeast is situated in the midst of bizarre rock formations. It was founded by the Despot Slav, the administrator of the area around Melnik, in the 12th or 13th century. The rather small iconostasis is a masterpiece of woodcarving. Prized frescoes from the beginning of the 17th cen-

The 24 double rows of windows catch the eye in the drawing room of the Kordopulov House

tury decorate the southern outside wall of *Sveta Bogorodica*, the main church.

In the village of *Karlanovo*, between Melnik and Rozhen Monastery, you'll find the small *Hotel Vodenicata* ('Watermill', *tel. 07437 22 31* | *Budget)* with a first-class *mehana*.

SOFIA

⫸ MAP INSIDE BACK COVER
(130 C1) *(𝑀 C5)* **'Serdica is my Rome!', Constantine the Great is once said to have exclaimed in utter delight. That was in the 4th century and he was referring to the settlement which at that time formed the centre of the Roman province of Thracia.**

Today, if you wander through the streets of Sofia (also written as Sofija) with its 1.4 million inhabitants, you'll only be able to unearth isolated traces of its turbulent history. Look out for remains from Roman times in central locations, for example in the ● *Serdika* subway under the former Communist Party headquarters, in the ruins of the eastern fortification wall dating from the 2nd century, and in the courtyard of the Sheraton Hotel where the 4th-century St George Rotunda lies hidden away. There are also countless exhibits in the main museums documenting the history of a city which, during its various ups and downs, has experienced many times of greatness. However, the picture the city presents gives the impression of an unusual mixture, somehow indifferent to history, collated over the last 100 years, a picture in which a handful of magnificent historic buildings and a few beautiful examples

For a holiday with a cultural angle Sofia is the perfect place – do pay a visit to the National Theatre

of Bulgarian architecture dating from around the turn of the last century stand out like colourful dots.

Today Sofia is the absolute centre of Bulgaria and, in a country with such a strong tradition of centralised structure, this doesn't apply only to the areas of government and administration. Though non-Sofians may turn up their noses when they hear it, much of what is of cultural interest is concentrated here – the main museums, the galleries which are the grandest, but at the same time most open to innovation, the best theatres, plus the top choirs and orchestras. Sofia also assumes the role of trendsetter in more prosaic matters. If you want to know what's in at the moment on the Bulgarian youth scene in terms of lifestyle and everyday culture, then you should head to Bulevard Vitosha and

some parts of the park outside the Palace of Culture early on a Friday or Saturday evening.

> **WHERE TO START?**
> **Ploshtad Sveta Nedelja (U C3) (*ℳ c3*):** the best starting point which is easy to get to by Metro (Serdika station) or tram lines 1, 2, 7 and 18 (Ploshtad Sveta Nedelja stop). If travelling to Sofia by car, use an underground car park at the Serdika station but bear in mind that traffic jams are an everyday occurrence and it makes more sense to use public transport or taxi to get into the centre.

SIGHTSEEING

BORISOVA GRADINA (BORIS' GARDEN) (U E–F 5–6) (*ℳ e–f 5–6*)

This is the place to come for a Sunday walk: the largest park in Sofia. *Off Bulevard Tsar Osvoboditel*

CENTRALNA EVREJSKA SINAGOGA (SYNAGOGUE) (U C2) (*ℳ c2*)

The largest synagogue on the Balkan peninsula was completed in 1910 and restored a few years ago. If there are members of the community present, they will show visitors round on payment of an entry fee of 2 leva. In the *Parish Hall (Bulevard Alexandar Stamboliiski 50 | 5th floor| Mon–Fri 9am–midday and 2–5pm)* you can see the permanent exhibition 'The Rescue of the Bulgarian Jews 1941–1944'. *Ulitsa Ekzarh Josif 16*

DZHAMIJA BANJA BASHI (BATHS MOSQUE) (U C2) (*ℳ c2*)

This mosque is the last remaining one for faithful Muslims in the capital. During the anti-Turk campaigns in the socialist era it was abandoned and only brought back into use at the beginning of the 1990s. The building, designed by the renowned Turkish architect Hadzhi Mimar Sinan, was completed in 1576. In the immediate vicinity you'll find the mineral baths which are no longer used but water from the mineral springs is sold. What is an absolute must is the restored *Market Hall (Centralni Hali* or *Halite)* on the opposite side of the road. *Bulevard Knjaginja Marija Luiza*

GRADSKA GRADINA (CITY GARDEN)
(U C–D3) (*ஹ c–d3*)

This is a green oasis, the ideal place to have a rest and get a breath of fresh air. It's also a popular meeting place for chess players. *Right in the centre, on Ulitsa Vasil Levski*

NACIONALEN ARCHEOLOGICHESKI MUZEJ (NATIONAL ARCHAEOLOGICAL MUSEUM) (U C3) (*ஹ c3*)

Opposite the president's official residence, where you can observe a sort of changing of the guard every hour, the National Archaeological Museum is housed in the Grand Mosque. Even though it's had to hand over some of its prized treasures to other museums, it's still certainly worthwhile having a look at the exhibition of articles of everyday life, weapons and jewellery once used by Thracians, Romans and Greeks. *Ulitsa Saborna 2 (by the Plostad Aleksandar Batenberg) | Tue–Sun 10am–midday and 2–5pm*

NACIONALEN ISTORICHESKI MUZEJ (NATIONAL MUSEUM OF HISTORY) ●
(O) (*ஹ C5*)

It's not all that easy to find the country's largest and most prestigious museum of Bulgarian history, as it is housed in the Boyana Residence adjacent to the president's official residence. Extending over three floors, it presents the story of the territory which is now Bulgaria and explains how that story has evolved over the past 2000 years. There are also some 22,000 exhibits for you to look at in the impressive premises of the former Zhivkov residence. The museum attracted worldwide attention with its 'Thracian Gold' exhibition; however, the Thracian goldsmiths' artistic masterpieces (dating probably from the turn of the 13th to the 12th century BC) are often loaned out for touring exhibitions. *Ulitsa Vitoshko Lale 16 | daily 9.30am–5pm | tel. 02 9 55 42 80 (Excursions/guided tours) | www.history museum.org | Bus no. 63 and 111 (see also sights in the surrounding area)*

NACIONALNA HUDOZHESTVENA GALERIJA (NATIONAL ART GALLERY)
(U D3) (*ஹ d3*)

This magnificent building, erected in the 16th century, was first used as a *konak*, the official seat of the Ottoman administration, and it was here that the trial of the Bulgarian national hero Vasil Levski was held. After liberation from Ottoman domination, the building was twice extended and converted and functioned as the imperial castle during the monarchy. Since 1954 it has been home to the National Gallery. The collection of Bulgarian art from the middle of the 19th century to the present day is no less attractive than the building itself. *Ploshtad Aleksandar Battenberg | Tue–Sun 10.30am–6pm*

INSIDERTIP ROTONDA SVETI GEORGI (ST GEORGE ROTUNDA) (U C3) (*ஹ c3*)

The rotunda is situated in the inner courtyard of the Sheraton Hotel and is thought to be the oldest surviving building in Sofia. It was built at the beginning of the

4th century during the rule of the Roman emperor Constantine the Great on the site of a former Roman baths complex. The rotunda was originally used by the Romans as a place of ritual, then by the Slavs as a Christian church, later by the

claimed more than 120 lives and more than 500 were injured. The badly damaged building was completely rebuilt in 1931. Even today it has not been unambiguously established whether the leaders of the Communist Party were respon-

The National Museum of History in Sofia has many treasures on view

Turks as a mosque and finally, when Bulgaria became a country in its own right, once more as a Christian church. Frescoes dating from the 14th century rank among the most impressive wall paintings with Baroque elements in Bulgaria. *Entrance from Ulitsa Saborna*

SVETA NEDELJA (ST NEDELYA CHURCH) (U C3) (𝓜 c3)

This church, built between 1856 and 1863, has attracted attention, not so much for its cultural treasures as for its temporal features and the political events it has witnessed. It's worth a visit, if only for the bright and not at all pretentious radiance it emanates.

In April 1925 a bomb attack in the church

sible for the attack, though they always vehemently denied it. They later used the church for their own purposes and the cupola housed an office of the secret police up to the end of the 1980s. *Ploshtad Sveta Nedelja*

SVETA SOFIJA (ST SOPHIA CHURCH) (U E3) (𝓜 e3)

The second oldest of the surviving church buildings is dedicated to the saint who gave the city its name. It was erected on the highest point in the centre of the settlement in the 6th century. Even during the Ottoman period, when the church was used as a mosque, its external appearance remained unchanged The cross-domed basilica with three naves and three altars is a unique example in Bulgaria of the severe monumentality of classical Byzantine architecture. On its eastern side is situated the grave of the Bulgarian national poet Ivan Vazov, whose statue in the nearby park – he's holding a book in his hand – is not to be missed. *Ploshtad Aleksandar Nevski*

Impressive – the St Alexander Nevsky Cathedral

SVETI ALEKSANDAR NEVSKI (ST ALEXANDER NEVSKY CATHEDRAL)
★ (U E3) (𝄞 e3)

Many non-Bulgarians who are much travelled in the Balkans consider the cathedral to be the finest 20th-century building on the Balkan peninsula. The church was erected on the highest point in the city in honour of the soldiers who fell in the Russo-Turkish War of 1877–78 and as a token of gratitude for the post-war separation of Bulgaria from the Ottoman Empire. Alexander II, the Russian tsar at that time, has ever since been honoured in Bulgaria as 'Tsar Osvoboditel' (King of Liberation). Not far from the cathedral, directly opposite the National Assembly building (Narodno Sabranie), a 14-m high monument, created by the Italian sculptor Arnoldo Zocchi and depicting the tsar mounted on his horse, is further evidence of this veneration.

The church took its name from Alexander Nevsky, the tsar's patron saint and a Moscow grand duke in the 13th century. It was designed by the Petersburg architect Alexander Pomeransev and building work started in 1904, continuing with minor interruptions until 1913. It was not until eleven years later in 1924 that the church was consecrated.

As you approach from Bulevard Tsar Osvoboditel, the first impression created when the south side comes into view is particularly striking and the two cupolas overlaid with gold leaf will really catch your eye. The Bulgarian government who commissioned the building stipulated that the church must be able to accommodate 5000 people. Inside, the fascination lies not so much with the outstanding individual items but rather with the works of art as a whole. The most celebrated Russian and Bulgarian masters at the turn of the century are represented here with murals, icons and mosaics.

The crypt houses a permanent exhibition of more than 200 icons, frescoes and printed icons by Bulgarian masters predominantly from the 18th and 19th century. But the exhibition also includes works from the 12th to the 17th century. The ● cathedral choir sings in the cathedral on Sundays and religious holidays during the church service and the building boasts outstanding acoustics. The music is always purely choral music, sung with no musical accompaniment. *Ploshtad Aleksander Nevski | daily 7am–7pm | Crypt: Tue–Sun 10am–6pm*

SVETI NIKOLAJ CHUDOTVORETS (CHURCH OF ST NICHOLAS THE MIRACLE MAKER) (U D3) (*m d3*)

You cannot fail to appreciate why the building, completed in 1914, is called the 'Russian Church'. With its five golden domes, it presents itself as a light and multi-coloured imitation of the Moscow architecture of the 17th century, with murals in the style of the Novgorod School of Painting. The church owes its existence to a Russian diplomat's concerns about his spiritual salvation because Semontovski-Kurilo, the Petersburg ambassador from 1908 to 1911, did not consider the Bulgarian church sufficiently orthodox for religious services to be held there. *Bulevard Tsar Osvoboditel 3*

FOOD & DRINK

CHEVERMETO (0) (*m 0*)

Every evening a lamb is roasted over an open fire in front of the guests. Heads of state and royalty have dined here. There's a large selection of wines and brandies, and Bulgarian live music and dancing to enjoy. *Bulevard Cherni Vrah 31 | www.chevermeto-bg.com | Moderate–Expensive*

CORNER BISTRO (U C4) (*m c4*)

Modern restaurant serving Mediterranean and European cuisine. There are power sockets by every table, a particularly useful feature for internet users. *Ulitsa Hristo Belchev 29 | Moderate*

FLOCAFE LOUNGE BAR ● (U C3) (*m c3*)

Popular meeting place with lots of specialist coffees, sweets and small dishes, it boasts a smart, modern interior decor and in the summer you can sit in the garden. *Ploshtad Sveta Nedelja 3*

FUNKY KITCHEN (U D4) (*m d4*)

Modern restaurant serving international cuisine. There's a bar in the cellar. It's a popular meeting place for young people. *Ulitsa Stefan Karadzha 26 | Budget–Moderate*

INSIDER TIP HADHIDRAGANOVITE KASHTI (0) (*m 0*)

A place to enjoy traditional cuisine, specialities from the grill and Bulgarian folk music as well. The restaurant complex consists of four restored houses from the Revival period. *Ulitsa Kozloduj 75 | www.kashtite.com | Moderate*

MANASTIRSKA MAGERNIZA (U C5) (*m c5*)

In the 'Monastery Kitchen' they serve food based on monastic recipes from all over Bulgaria. Guests are greeted in the traditional manner with an offering of bread and salt. *Ulitsa Han Asparuh 67 | www.magernitsa.com | Expensive*

INSIDER TIP SUN MOON ORGANIC RESTAURANT AND BAKERY ☺ (U B4) (*m b4*)

The food is vegetarian, the fruit and vegetables being provided by local smallholders. You can buy different types of wholemeal bread from the bakery. *Ulitsa Gladston 18b | www.sunmoon.bg | Budget–Moderate*

SHOPPING

By Bulgarian standards Sofia has always been able to offer particularly good opportunities for shopping. The main shops and most compact shopping areas are situated in and around *Bulevard Vitosha, Ulitsa Pirotska, Ulitsa Rakovski* and *Ulitsa Graf Ignatiev* (especially around *Ploshtad Slavejkov*). There are countless fashion boutiques for the discerning customer. The largest department store is *TSUM (Bulevard Knjaginja Marija Luiza 2 | www.tzum.bg)* where there are lots of outlets selling international fashion and luxury goods labels. You will find antique and second-hand shops at the large flea market outside the Alexander Nevsky Cathedral and, in the immediate vicinity, in Ulitsa Parizh, you can buy copies of icons and paintings.

Delightful handicrafts and souvenirs are available in the *Siana Art Centre (www.siana-art.com),* and in the subways under the TSUM department store original paintings, national costumes and ● essence of rose are all for sale. You'll find items made of marble and semi-precious stones at *Bulevard Tsar Osvoboditel 10,* and crystal and porcelain at *Bulevard Vitosha 8*. The smaller shops around *Ploshtad Slavejkov* sell attractive leather clothing and furs as well as hand bags and, for their size, they stock an above-average range of leather goods. If you're looking for expensive jewellery and watches, have a look round in *El Grado (Bulevard Vitosha 61)* or in *Oxette (Bulevard Vitosha 9)*. Classical music lovers will be able to pick up first-class recordings in the specialist music bookshop *Bulgarian Composer (Ulitsa Ivan Vazov, next to the National Theatre)* and you can get folk and pop music from the street traders on *Bulevard Vitosha* and *Ploshtad Slavejkov.*

Zhenski Pazar, the central fruit and vegetable market, is on *Bulevard Stefan Stambolov.* In the renovated market halls *(Centralni Hali* or *Halite, Bulevard Knjaginja Marija Luiza 25)* there are more than 100 stalls selling a great variety of fresh food and delicacies from 7am till midnight. It's also a great place to observe a way of life that hasn't changed in centuries, with people going about their daily chores and haggling with the traders.

The sale of certified organic products is still in its infancy in Bulgaria. But in the organic food shop ☺ *Smesen Magazin* there's not only a café, but you can also buy organic cosmetics, the products coming from small family businesses throughout Bulgaria *(Ulitsa Aksakov 22 | www.zoya.bg)*. Some of the large supermarkets sell organic produce with various Bulgarian brand names. The organic food shop run by the *Bio Bulgaria* label, for example, is situated outside the city centre *(Journalist Square 1)*.

ENTERTAINMENT

Issued weekly, the INSIDER TIP *Guide Programata (also available in English | www.programata.bg)* provides an overview of the main addresses and cultural events. You can pick up a copy in restaurants, pubs and cinemas.

Tickets for major events are available at the advance booking office in the *NDK* Palace of Culture, the largest culture and congress centre in south-eastern Europe. **(U B6)** *(ɯ b6)* tel. 02 9 16 63 69 | daily 9am–7pm | www.ndk.bg

There's a large number of live clubs to choose from in Sofia, but amongst the best are *Swinging Hall* **(U E6)** *(ɯ e6) (Bulevard Dragan Tsankov 8)* with regularly changing live bands, and the Coolhouse *Bibliotekata* **(U E3)** *(ɯ e3) (Bulevard Vasil Levski 88)*. As for western style discos, the city has made a massive effort to catch up in recent years. The *Chervilo* (in English, lipstick) is and remains a hot tip **(U D3)** *(🗺 d3) (Bulevard Tsar Osvoboditel | www.chervilo.com)* and you'll find folklore programmes in lots of restaurants in the city.

rant with garden. *31 rooms | Ulitsa Han Asparuh 65 | tel. 02 9 89 89 98 www.dit erhotel.com | Expensive*

HOTEL LOZENETZ (0) *(🗺 0)*

This is a new, elegant building not far

The Swinging Hall – the place to hear live music

WHERE TO STAY

GRAND HOTEL SOFIA (U C4) *(🗺 c4)*

Luxury hotel in the centre of the city – with gourmet restaurant, fitness centre and piano bar. It also has a notable collection of over 400 original oil paintings! *109 rooms, 13 suites | Ulitsa Gurko 1 | tel. 02 8 11 08 00 | www.grandhotelsofia.bg | Expensive*

 **INSIDER TIP ▶ HOTEL DITER**
(U C5) *(🗺 d5)*

Quiet with a central location. This family hotel is located in the renovated house, where Todor G. Vlaykov, a Bulgarian writer and politician, lived in the first half of the 20th century. It has its own restau-

from the city centre and provides free wi-fi internet access and a comfortable restaurant serving traditional Bulgarian cuisine. It has a summer garden. *31 rooms and apartments | Bulevard Sveti Naum | tel. 02 9 65 44 44 | www. lozenetzhotel.com | Moderate–Expensive*

INTERNET HOSTEL SOFIA
(U C3) *(🗺 s3)*

Very central location in a large flat on the 2nd floor of an apartment block. Individually furnished, the bedrooms have a total of ten beds. Non-smoking apartment. *Ulitsa Alabin 50A | tel. 0889 13 82 98 | www.hostelz.com/hostel/17024-Internet-Hostel-Sofia | Budget*

KERVAN HOSTEL (U E2) (⌘ e2)
Quiet with a central location, it's just three minutes on foot to the St Alexander Nevsky Cathedral. Individually furnished, you can make your own meals in the small kitchen and meet other guests. It also has a summer garden and provides internet access. | *Ulitsa Rosica 3* | *tel. 02 9 83 94 28* | *www.kervanhostel.com* | *Budget*

MAXI PARK HOTEL & SPA (0) (⌘ 0)
The complex is located at the foot of Vitosha Massif outside the city centre. It has a very extensive spa centre with a 25-metre swimming pool, a fully-equipped fitness centre, 7 outdoor and 2 indoor tennis courts and a choice of restaurants. At weekends, prices are lower than in the week. *96 rooms* | *Ulitsa Simeonovsko Shose 111* | *tel. 02 8 92 00 00* | *www.maxisofia.com* | *Moderate–Expensive*

MORIAH HOTEL FLATS
Live like you do at home: seven holiday apartments with one, two or three bedrooms. All the apartments enjoy a central location and are comfortably furnished. *Tel. 02 9 86 12 46 and 0 88 94 80 01* | *www.moriahflats.com* | *Budget*

SHERATON SOFIJA HOTEL BALKAN (U C3) (⌘ c3)
An island of luxury in the very heart of the city, right next to the residence of the Bulgarian state president. The building was erected in the mid-1950s as the Hotel Balkan. After a complete refurbishment in the mid-1980s it was taken over to become the first Sheraton hotel in eastern Europe. Royalty, state presidents and VIPs have stayed here. The hotel is a member of the Luxury Collection of Starwood Hotels & Resorts. *173 rooms, 15 apartments* | *Ploshtad Sveta Nedelja 5* | *tel. 02 9 81 65 41* | *www.sheratonsofia.com* | *Expensive*

BALKAN TOURIST INFORMATION (U C3) (⌘ c3)
Bulevard Tsar Osvoboditel 4 | *tel. 02 9 87 51 92* | *www.balkantourist.bg*

BRITISH AIRWAYS BULGARIA CONTACT (U B5) (⌘ b5)
49 Patriarch Evtimii Blvd., 1st floor, | *tel. 359 2 954 7000* | *www.customercarecontacts.com/british-airways-bulgaria-contact-phone-address*

WHERE TO GO

BOYANA (130 C1) (⌘ C5)
Numerous top-ranking members of the Communist Party had villas built 8km/5mi south of the city centre, and Todor Zhivkov had the residence built which continues to be used as the official residence of the state president. The town has achieved greater historical importance through the ★ ● *Boyanskata Tsarkva*, a church from the 11th century bearing the town's name and included in Unesco's list of World Heritage Sites. In 1259 an annex with wonderful, expressive murals was added to the church. The frescoes include biblical scenes, pictures of spiritual and temporal leaders, together with realistic reflections of everyday life. They're considered to be the jewel in the crown of Bulgarian painting of the Middle Ages and are seen as precursors of the European Renaissance. Their creator is unknown but he's always referred to as the 'Master of Boyana'. *Ulitsa Boyansko ezero 1–3* | *April–Oct 9.30am–5.30pm, Nov–Mar 9am–5pm* | *Bus 64, 107* | *www.boyanachurch.org*

DRAGALEVTSI ⚜ (130 C1) (⌘ C5)
Only the church of the Dragalevtsi Monastery dating from the 14th century has

been preserved. The old watermill in the village has been renovated and it now houses the *Vodenitsata* restaurant *(tel. 02 9 67 10 58 | Moderate)* which serves traditional Bulgarian food, plus there's a fantastic view over the capital. Dragalevtsi is 10km/6mi from the centre of Sofia and is easy to get to using public transport: tram line 9 or 10 as far as the *Hladilnika stop*, then by bus no. 66.

tor below the Aleko centre and proceed from there on the chair lift. Afterwards stroll up to the peak or across the plateau *(Plato)* to the *Zlatni Mostove* ('Golden Bridges') where you'll find the so-called Stone River, huge boulders which look as though they're tumbling down the mountain. A detour to the ☀ *Kopitoto* complex with café, restaurant and panoramic view of Sofia takes one and a half

The church in Boyana – nothing special from the outside, but utterly enchanting inside

VITOSHA MOUNTAINS ★
(130 C1–2) (*∅ B–C5*)

The Sofians' local recreation area is to be found just 10km/6mi from the capital's centre. There are several possible ways of reaching the highest peak, the ☀ *Cherni Vrah* (,Black Peak', 2290m/7513ft). The direct ascent from Dragalevtsi takes several hours. But you can also take bus no. 66 as far as the Aleko winter sports centre and from there the summit is two hours away. A more relaxing way is to take the ● gondola lift from the Simeonovo area of the city to the Hotel Pros-

hours. From Zlatni Mostove take the taxi sharing service to get to the city district of Ovcha Kupel and from there catch tram no. 5 to get back to the centre. Vitosha is also an attractive destination for winter sports fans and there's snow from the end of December to the end of March. The ski resort has six ski runs of all degrees of difficulty with a length of 29km/18mi. The easiest way for skiers to get from Simeonovo to Aleko, where the ski runs are located, is on the gondola lift. *www.skivitosha.com*

VIDIN

(124 B1) *(∅ B1)* **The largest town (pop. 67,000) in the still underdeveloped north-western corner of Bulgaria, barely touched by tourism, is about 200km/125mi from Sofia.**

You can also get to Vidin from Romania by ferry across the Danube. A bridge across the river to the Romanian town of Calafat which people have been talking about for years is finally under construction, with people on both sides of the river hoping for an economic upturn generated by more tourism.

Vidin was founded in the 3rd century BC as a Roman settlement and it was an important Bulgarian fortress in the Middle Ages, not least because of its strategic location on the Danube. Even during the time of the Ottoman Empire the town was an important administrative and economic centre, which is why it was, over time, repeatedly occupied by Habsburg troops. You can still find traces of these times in the town of today.

SIGHTSEEING

INSIDERTIP BABA VIDA

The fortress on the banks of the Danube is Bulgaria's best preserved site from the Middle Ages. It was built between the 10th and the 14th century on the foundations of a Roman defence tower and its purpose was to protect the town. Before the Ottoman conquest it was also the residence of the last Bulgarian tsar Ivan Srazimir (1356–96). The walls, four defence towers and parts of the two-storey main building have been preserved. Countless Bulgarian and foreign films have been made in the fortress and in 2003 scenes from ‚The Lord of the Rings' were filmed here. A museum and a stage are part of the complex and at night it is impressively illuminated. *Daily 9am–6pm | 8 lv | www.babavida.vidin.net*

FOOD & DRINK

CLASSIC

Bulgarian and Italian specialities. *Ulitsa Tsar Aleksandar II 25 (opposite the river railway station) | Budget–Moderate*

MILANOVATA KASHTA

'The House of Milan', a family-run restaurant, is close to the Danube and serves traditional Bulgarian and international food. It has an enormous garden, perfect for hot summer nights, and boasts a great selection of wines. *Ulitsa Vela Peeva 36 | Budget–Moderate*

WHERE TO STAY

HOTEL ANA KRISTINA

An elegant hotel in the town gardens by the banks of the Danube in a listed, faithfully-restored building dating from the last century. With restaurant, Viennese salon, barbecue garden and swimming pool. *21 rooms | Ulitsa Baba Vida 2 | tel. 094 60 60 38 | anna-kristina.dir.bg | Moderate*

HOTEL VIDIN

The hotel with restaurant and beer garden is located in the town centre not far from the town gardens. *9 rooms | Ulitsa Knjaz Dondukov 15 | tel. 094 60 69 38 | www.hotelvidin.com | Budget*

INFORMATION

TOURIST INFORMATION CENTRE

Ploshtad Bdintsi 6 (in the art gallery next to the Disco Sky Club) | tel. 094 60 14 21 | www.vidin.bg

WHERE TO GO

BELOGRADCHISHKI SKALI (BELOGRADCHIK ROCKS) (124 A3) (*ω A2*)

The Belogradchik Rocks are located 50km/30mi south of Vidin. The huge rock formations which look like people, animals and castles all have names and histories which the travel guides there will be happy to supply. The remains of an old fortress used for defence purposes until 1885 lie strewn amongst the rocks.

INSIDERTIP PESHTERA MAGURA (MAGURA CAVE) (124 A2) (*ω A2*)

Magura, 45km/28mi southwest of Vidin, is one of the largest caves in Bulgaria with 2500m of subterranean labyrinths. The unique caverns are impressive above all by virtue of their colossal scale: more than 200m long, more than 50m wide and more than 20m high.

Archaeological excavations have shown that the cave was occupied as long as 7000 years ago, and large numbers of bones of various prehistoric species such as the cave bear and cave hyena have been discovered here. In the so-called *Portrait Gallery* prehistoric artists have drawn more than 700 religious ceremonies, deities and hunting scenes, creating unique works of prehistoric art. Some of the rock paintings have a relief-like effect. Because the air in this section was one degree warmer than in the rest of the cave (approx. 13°C/55°F), this was a location where bats liked to establish their colonies, and it was their droppings which were then used to create the wall paintings.

A Bronze Age calendar adorns the walls of the adjacent *Sun Room*.

Part of the cave is now used as a wine cellar where bottles of the only sparkling wine produced in Bulgaria following the Champagne-making process are stored. And in the large Triumph Hall the Vidin Philharmonic Orchestra occasionally performs concerts.

The wall paintings in the Magura Cave were produced using bat droppings

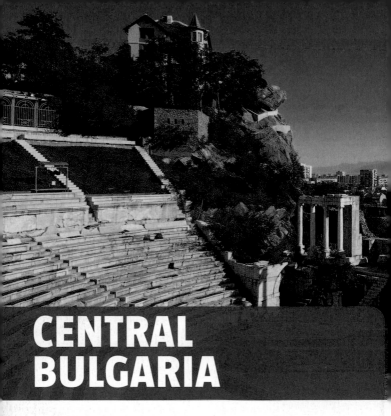

CENTRAL BULGARIA

The towns and villages in Central Bulgaria are characterised by different eras and cultures. Veliko Tarnovo and the surrounding area was the birthplace of the modern Bulgarian state, and everywhere in the central part of the Balkans you'll encounter evocations of the National Revival dating from the 18th and 19th century.

In Plovdiv there are lots of remains which recall the Thracian period and above all the fact that it was here during the Ottoman Empire that one of the centres of European Turkey was situated.

The central part of the Balkans and its mountains are lovely, readily accessible and negotiable. The best way to explore the area is from Veliko Tarnovo or Gabrovo, thereby killing two birds with one stone. The most compact concentration of listed towns and museums – such as Bozhentsi, Trjavna and Etara – is to be found in the environs of Gabrovo, and Rose Valley lies not far to the south. It's only Koprivshtitsa, halfway between Sofia and Plovdiv or Sofia and Gabrovo, which demands a longer journey, but this fairy-tale town will more than make up for that.

PLOVDIV

(132 B3) (*F6*) The city of Plovdiv today consists of two parts, the new city and the ★ *Old Town*. The jewel in the crown, the Old Town, is visible from quite a distance, rising up on the three

Thracians in Plovdiv and the birthplace of the National Revival in Veliko Tarnovo – history comes alive in Central Bulgaria

hills, **Nebet Tepe (Sentry Hill)**, **Dzhambaz Tepe (Ropedancer Hill)** and **Taksim Tepe (Watershed Hill)**.

A walk round the city will take you through the city's history, beginning with the settlement by the Thracians via the Roman and Ottoman periods up to the time of the National Revival in the 18th and 19th century, when the Bulgarians began to reflect on their own traditions. It was then that Plovdiv experienced another high point as a trading city, as evidenced by the many beautiful merchants'

WHERE TO START?

Start your tour through Plovdiv at **Ploshtad Tsentralen** (Central Square). You can get here from the railway and bus station on bus 26. In the new city there are pay car parks and the *Dedeman Trimontium Princess Hotel, Ulitsa Kapitan Raicho 2* offers further parking opportunities.

houses dating from the time of the National Revival. Today only 4500 of the total population of 350,000 live and work in the Old Town. It has the appearance of an inhabited open-air museum with picturesque houses bestowing an unmistakeable charm.

exhibits date from antiquity, from Thracian and Roman times. Of most interest here are the Bronze Age burial site from the region around Plovdiv, the bronze helmet from Brestovica dating from the Thracian period, as well as the Byzantine gold coins from the 12th century.

Sveti Sveti Konstantin i Elena – magnificent wall paintings

SIGHTSEEING

The city is full of winding streets, so first of all it's best to take a stroll through the streets and then to target the individual sights. Ruins from the Roman and Ottoman times are to be found in the *new city*, and lots of pretty cafés have sprung up on *Ploshtad Stefan Stambolov*.

ARCHEOLOGICHESKI MUZEJ (ARCHAEOLOGICAL MUSEUM)

The main exhibit in the archaeological museum is the gold treasure trove from Panagyurishte. It consists of nine vessels and weighs in total 6kg. Other significant

Ploshtad Saedinenie 1 | Tue–Sun 10am–5.30pm | www.archaeologicalmuseum plovdiv.org

DZHUMAJA DZHAMIJA (DZHUMAYA MOSQUE)

This mosque dates from the early 15th century. Inside are a series of ornate friezes with surahs of the Koran and the façade is decorated with a sun dial. *Ploshtad Dzhumaja*

ETNOGRAFSKI MUZEJ (ETHNOGRAPHIC MUSEUM)

There's an exhibition of craftwork dating from the Revival period on the lower floor of the stunningly beautiful *Agir Kujumdzhioglu House*. Rather more interesting than the collection of tools are the upper rooms with their displays of furnishings (lots of west and central European Baroque) and national costumes from the Rhodopes. Chamber music concerts are held in the museum courtyard in June and September. *Ulitsa Chomakov 2 | Tue–Sun 9am–midday and 1.30–5.30pm*

HISAR KAPIJA

The East Gate dates from the time of late antiquity when Plovdiv became a city (4th–1st century BC). *Ulitsa Tsanko Lavrenov*

RIMSKI FORUM (ROMAN FORUM)

The forum, covering an area of 27 acres, was designed during the reign of the Emperor Vespasian in the 1st century. Cobbled streets and foundations of individual buildings have been unearthed. *By the central square, between the Trimontium Princess Hotel and the main post office | 6 lv*

RIMSKI STADION (ROMAN STADIUM)

The stadium dates from the 2nd century and its exit and western part as well as the remains of rooms and a water main can still be seen. It once held 30,000 people and games were held every four years, based on the model of the Greek Olympics. The main disciplines were discus, javelin, running, long jump and wrestling. *Ploshtad Stambolijski*

ROMAN THEATRE �

The finest testament to antiquity is the theatre dating from the 2nd century. It was built by Emperor Marcus Aurelius and today can hold a good 3000 spectators. It offers a marvellous view of the Rhodopes. Classical theatre and concerts are performed here in May, June and September. *By the south side of the Dzhambaz Tepe, above the tunnel and the Ulitsa Ivajlo*

CITY WALL

Remains of the inner city wall of what was then Philippopolis (4th to 1st century BC) can be found by Nebet Tepe Hill in the park of the same name.

INSIDER TIP ▶ SVETI SVETI KONSTANTIN I ELENA

The church was built between 1830 and 1832. The well-known wood carver Joan Pashkula created the gilded exterior wall and numerous icons are the work of the important painter Zahari Zograf. *Corner Ulitsa Gorki/Starinna*

REVIVAL ARCHITECTURE
Above all it's the 19th-century buildings that give the Old Town its interest and vitality. The richly decorated façade of the *Agir Kujumdzhioglu House* dating from 1847 is one of the most frequently photographed features in the city, and today it houses the *Ethnographic Museum (Ulitsa Dr. Chomakov 2 | Summer Tue–Sun 9am–12.30pm and 1.30–6pm, winter Tue–Sun 9am–12.30pm and 1.30–5pm)*. The *Georgiadi House*, a striking building with a façade of bay windows and a projecting roof, houses the *National Revival Museum (Ulitsa Canko Lavrenov 1 | Mon–Sat 9am–midday and 2–5pm)*. The INSIDERTIP *Hindlian House (Ulitsa Artin Gidikov 11 | Mon–Fri 9am–midday and 1–6.30pm)* used to belong to an affluent Armenian merchant's family and boasts arguably the most splendid interior design and furnishings in the city. The ● INSIDERTIP *Nedkovich House*, also a merchant's house, was built in 1863 and

is reminiscent of an Italian palazzo. The interior is magnificent, especially in the ladies' salon. *Ulitsa Tsanko Lavrenov 3 | Mon–Fri 9.30am–midday and 12.30–6pm*

FOOD & DRINK

ALAFRANGITE
Here you can eat in a magnificent building dating from the 19th century. It has an inviting garden and serves Bulgarian and European food, accompanied by live piano music. *Ulitsa Kiril Nektariev 17 | Moderate*

ART CAFE PHILIPOPOLIS ⚓
Small restaurant with terrace – in the Old Town. Fine view of Plovdiv while you eat. *Ulitsa Saborna 29 | Budget–Moderate*

GLADIATORI
Bulgarian and international cuisine, large garden. *Ulitsa Dimitar Talev 87 | www.gladiatori.info | Moderate*

ODEON
Restaurant by the Roman Forum, ornately furnished. Bulgarian and central Euro-

Revival buildings define Plovdiv's appearance

pean cuisine, summer terrace. *Ulitsa Otec Paisij 40* | *Moderate–Expensive*

PALDIN

This grandest building in the Old Town serves a wide range of Bulgarian dishes. *Ulitsa Knjaz Ceretelev 3* | *Moderate–Expensive*

INSIDER TIP **YEREVAN**

Spicy Bulgarian and Armenian cuisine, simple furnishing. One speciality of the restaurant is *anush abur*, a sweet soup made of wheat and dried fruits. *Ulitsa Otec Paisij 29* | *Budget*

SHOPPING

The workshops in *Stramna Lane* are home to many of the city's artisans, such as coppersmiths, furriers and cobblers, who deploy skills acquired over generations. Their products decorate the walls and windows of the sometimes tiny shops like items in a museum, enticing passers-by to come in and buy something.

ENTERTAINMENT

Plovdiv has plenty to offer in terms of classical music and theatre. The *Concert Hall* where the City Philharmonic is the resident orchestra is situated on *Ploshtad Tsentralen* and the *Opera* on *Bulevard Sasho Dimitrov 23*. A renowned *Festival of Chamber Music* is held in June every two years (always in the odd years). The *concerts* are given *in the courtyard of the Ethnographic Museum* where local artists make guest appearances throughout the summer (tickets for musical events in *Ulitsa Knjaz Aleksandar 35*). *Classical theatre* is performed in the *main building* in *Ulitsa Knjaz Aleksandar 36* and – in a particularly impressive setting – the *Ro-*

man Theatre. Lively centres for the coffee house and bar culture have established themselves in *Ulitsa Knjaz Aleksandar,* around *Ploshtad Stambolijski* and in the Old Town. The *Brilyantin* club *(7.30am– 4am | Bulevard Maria Luiza 3)* has a modern interior and offers pleasant surroundings for a beer or a cocktail.

WHERE TO STAY

BULGARIA

This hotel guarantees a comfortable night's sleep in the city centre. *60 rooms | Ulitsa Patriarch Evtimij 13 | tel. 032 63 34 03 and 032 63 35 99 | www.hotel-bulgaria.net* | *Expensive*

INSIDER TIP **HEBROS** ☺

This is a small, charming hotel in the Old Town, very beautifully equipped. The restaurant with Slow Food Club is also recommended, and the emphasis is on cooking that uses mainly local ingredients. *6 rooms, 4 apartments | Ulitsa Konstantin Stoilov 51a | tel. 032 26 01 80 and 032 62 59 29 | www.hebros-hotel.com* | *Expensive*

PARKHOTEL IMPERIAL

Comfortable hotel a little way out of the city centre. With car park, fitness centre and a 5-a-side football pitch. *114 rooms | Ulitsa Arhitect Kamen Petkov 1 a | tel. 032 60 07 30 | www.hotelimperialbg.com* | *Budget–Moderate*

RENAISSANCE

City centre hotel in a renovated building dating from the 19th century; spacious, individually-equipped rooms decorated in various colours. Car park, restaurant and coffee house. *5 rooms | Ploshtad Vazrazhdane 1 II | tel. 032 26 69 66 | www.renaissance-bg.com* | *Budget–Moderate*

TOURIST INFORMATION CENTRE
*Ploshtad Sveta Nedelya 1 | tel. 032
65 67 94 | www.plovdiv.bg*
Several videos of the sights are available
at virtual.plovdiv.bg
*Ulitsa Saborna 22 | tel. 032 62 04 53 |
www.plovdiv-tour.info*

PLOVDIV GUIDE
*Ulitsa Ravnishta 6 | tel. 032 64 07 50 |
www.plovdivguide.com*

WHERE TO GO

ASENOVGRAD (132 B3–4) *(Ⓜ F7)*
Highway no. 86 from Plovdiv to Smolyan
via Asenovgrad is one of the most attractive routes in the Rhodopes. In Asenovgrad (pop. 50,000), situated
20km/12mi to the south, there is the
INSIDERTIP *Asenova Krepost* fortress,
one of the oldest castles in Bulgaria. The
fortress complex at the end of a picturesque valley in the foothills of the Rhodopes is a particularly impressive sight,
because of the exposed position of the
two-storey ⚡ *Sveta Bogoroditsa Petrich-
ka church*. Due to its location in the
mountains the town enjoys a very pleasant climate – ideal for the local vine
growing industry.

BACHKOVSKI MANASTIR (BACHKOVO MONASTERY) ★ (132 B4) *(Ⓜ F7)*
Situated a good 20km/12mi to the south
near Asenovgrad in the heart of the Rhodope Mountains, this monastery is the
second largest in Bulgaria, after the Rila
monastery. It is also second in terms of
its significance for architecture, art and
the spiritual life of the country. The monastery was founded in 1083 by the Geor-
gian brothers Grigori and Abasi Bakuriani
who had managed to gain autonomous

status for the community from the Byzantine emperor. From the 12th to the 14th
century Bulgarian and Byzantine posses-
sion alternated until in the middle of the
14th century the Bulgarian tsar, Ivan
Aleksandar, established his power over
the Rhodopes.
The site's oldest building is the ossuary, a
church vault which was built at the time
of the monastery's foundation. The rest
dates essentially from the reconstruction
in the 17th century. The main *Sveta Bogorodica* church was erected as a crossed-
dome church in 1604. This church is the
Bulgarians' only surviving place of worship dating from the time of the National
Revival.
The most significant wall paintings adorn
St Nicholas Church in the monastery's
southern courtyard. The works, completed in 1840, have gone down in the history of Bulgarian art as the first significant work by the master Zahari Zograf.
This is where you'll find the first self-por-
trait of a Bulgarian painter, the first
genuine genre paintings and realistic
portrayals of landscape, as well as, for
the first time, criticism of authority, the
Plovdiv notables clearly recognisable
amongst the sinners at the Last Judge-
ment.

KOPRIVSHTITSA ★ (132 A1) *(Ⓜ E5)*
This is a lovely valley in the Sredna Gora
central mountains. Surrounded by forested slopes and penetrated by two rivers, it contains a village of winding
streets with a virtually endless collection
of fairy tale cottages, churches, wells and
bridges from the 18th and 19th century.
The appearance Koprivshtitsa presents is
one of a unique village which has es-
caped the ravages of time. Advice and
information is available at the *Tourist
Information Centre | Ploshtad 20 april 6 |
tel. 07184 21 91 | www.koprivshtitsa.info*

LESHTEN (131 E5) (*D8*)

In the western part of the Rhodopes, 15km/9mi and 20km/12mi north of Goce Delchev, lie the villages of Kovachevitsa and Leshten, where time seems to have

sports centre, is situated just under 90km/56mi south of Plovdiv, at the foot of the Snezhanka peak. Pamporovo is the southernmost ski resort in Bulgaria. From the end of December to the end of March the snow conditions are good

Vault in Bachkovo Monastery – the monastery was founded in 1083

stood still. There are houses made of wood and stone, narrow cobbled alleys and both villages enjoy full protected status. In the surrounding area you can ride, walk and fish. In Kovachevitsa: *The White House family hotel | 9 rooms | tel. 0889 8 88 63 42 | ecotourbg.com | Budget*. For where to stay in Leshten: *tel. 0888 54 46 51 | leshten.hit.bg | Moderate*

PAMPOROVO AND TRIGRAD
(132 B5) (*E8*)

At a height of 1620m/5315ft, the Pamporovo tourist complex, a popular winter

both for downhillers and cross-country skiers. The mountain ski runs are 23 km/14mi in length and are graded easy to medium hard, which makes Pamporovo very well-suited to families with children *(www.pamporovo.net)*.

If you enjoy walking in the mountains but prefer gentler slopes, then you're better off here in the summer than in the Rila or Pirin Mountains. The sun shines almost throughout the year, and the meadows covered in flowers, peaceful lakes, rushing streams and the fragrance of wild berries and herbs everywhere will whet your appetite for countryside tours. There are several hotels, and the *Malina Holiday Village (tel. 03021 83 88)* with 30 wooden chalets can also provide living quarters. If you're travelling alone, you can get better value for money by staying in Smolyan, a small town to the south, or in Stoikite, a village to the west. The *Grand Hotel Murgavec* can be recommended as a lovely hotel in summer and winter *(76 rooms | tel. 0309 5 83 66 | www.murgavets-bg.com | Moderate).*

A day trip, away from the centres of tourism, includes one of the most beautiful spots in Bulgaria. Follow the road west heading towards Dospat and after about 30km/20mi, in the village of Teshel, turn left towards Trigrad (131 F5) (*׻ E8*). As the road now gets narrower, the rocks by the roadside get higher. After another 10km/6mi you reach the narrowest section: INSIDERTIP *Trigradsko Zhdrelo* (Trigrad Gorge) with the ● *Djavolkso Garlo* (Devil's Throat) caves and *Haramijskata*. In Djavolkso Garlo there is a subterrane-

an, 60-m high waterfall. Legend has it that this is the place from where Orpheus descended into the underworld to find his beloved Eurydice. There are several 30-minute guided tours every day. Haramijskata cave can only be entered by joining a guided tour, and the cave walk is more demanding, taking four to five hours, but it's a real adventure if you're a sports enthusiast. *Information, guides and equipment in Trigrad, Hotel Silivrjak | tel. 03040 2 20*

For a place to stay the night in Trigrad there's the *Arkan Han* Hotel *(15 rooms | Trigrad village | www.arkantours.com | Budget),* a new comfortable hotel with traditional architecture, which also offers horseriding, cave walks and archaeological tourism.

ROZOVA DOLINA (ROSE VALLEY)
(132 B–C1) (*׻ F–G5*)

Rose oil is one of Bulgaria's world-famous products, and it is extracted in the valley of petals. Bulgaria produces 70 percent of the world's rose oil, the climate here being ideal for rose cultivation. It goes without saying that the best time to visit the valley is when the roses are in bloom *(end of May/beginning of June),* when the fragrance and the colours are wonderful. The rose petals are harvested by hand, from sunrise till midday at the latest. This keeps the petals fresh and they lose none of their moisture.

The Rose Festival is celebrated at the start of June when the locals take part in harvesting traditions with music and dance. A rose queen is also chosen. The festival with its processions and bazaars lasts several days and is held in *Kazanlak* and *Karlovo*, but there are also celebrations in the smaller towns. In Kazanlak, the capital of the Rose Valley, there's a Rose Museum, where visitors can buy rose oil, rose cosmetics and jam, and

LOW BUDGET

▶ Village tourism *(Selski Turizam)*: a holiday on a farm is an inexpensive alternative way of getting to know the country. Meals are also often provided. *www.ruralbulgaria.com | selskiturizam.start.bg*

▶ Homemade dishes, also takeaways, are available at very reasonable prices in the *Kopcheto* food shop in Plovdiv. The menu is huge, but don't confuse it with the Kopcheto restaurant which is located nearby. *Ulitsa Trakija 48, behind Alliance Hotel | www.kopcheto.net*

A good reason for a party – the roses are harvested late May, early June

taste liqueurs and brandy made from rose petals. Other displays show how the petals are processed. *Kulata Museum Complex | Ulitsa Mirska (in the town district of Kulata) | daily 9am–5.30pm*

In addition to rose growing, vines are also grown in Rose Valley, the Kadarka Rose Valley wine variety taking its name from here.

Without the splendour of the young roses, the towns in the valley are unfortunately greyer and less attractive than many travel guides would have you believe. The best place to start off on a visit to Rose Valley is from the town of *Kazanlak* (pop. 58,000), 120km/75mi northeast of Plovdiv. This is famous for the *Thracian Tomb* in *Tjulbeto Park* which dates from the 4th century BC. Discovered by accident in 1944, it has been listed by Unesco as a World Heritage Site. In order to protect the original, it's not open to the public,

but some 50m away there is a replica *(daily 8.30am–5.30pm)*. In the very centre of the town is the *Hotel Kazanlak (187 rooms | Ulitsa Rozova Dolina 2 | tel. 0431 2 02 06 | www.hotelkazanlak-bg.com | Budget)*, the top address in town.

The Rose Valley, and in particular the small town of *Kalofer,* is the best starting point for excursions into the Sredna Gora Mountains. The biggest attraction of Kalofer is the *birthplace of Hristo Botev* (1848–76), the poet, utopian socialist and active revolutionary, who was killed at Vraca on a mission shortly after the 1876 April uprising against the Turkish rulers.

Vasil Levski was born in *Karlovo* (pop. 29,000), and today his *birthplace* is a museum *(Ulitsa General Karzov 57 | daily 8.30am–1pm and 2–5pm)*. A walk through the old town is well worth the effort and will pass by some restored 19th-century buildings.

VELIKO TARNOVO

(126 C5) (𝄞 H4) ★ **To the south the Balkans, to the north the Danube lowlands, down in the valley the meandering Jantre River, and in the middle lies the city of Veliko Tarnovo.**

The shape of the town is reminiscent of a large bird which, with wings extended, has settled on the rock terraces. It is one of Bulgaria's finest towns. Large parts of the picturesque Old Town are protected. This beautifully situated town (pop. 66,000) can look back on a 5000-year history of settlement. For two centuries, from the end of the 12th to the end of the 14th century, it was the capital of the

WHERE TO START?
Ploshtad Tsar Ivan Asen II: this square by the bridge over the River Jantra is a good starting point to visit Veliko Tarnovo. Buses 20, 50 and 110 stop here. The stop is called Sveti chetireset machenitsi. For those travelling by car, there are parking spaces round the *Sveti chetireset machenitsi* and *Sveti Peter i Pavel* churches.

Second Bulgarian Empire and for a short time, after the fragmentation of the Ottoman Empire, also of the new Bulgarian state. Veliko Tarnovo was the birthplace of lots of important schools of literature, architecture and painting, and the home of famous

Veliko Tarnovo stands on a hillside

figures associated with the National Revival.

The remains of Tsaravets Castle and the Patriarchal Cathedral on Tsarevets Hill are testament to the town's former role as a capital, as is the labyrinth of streets in the old quarter north and south of Ulitsa Dimitar Blagoev, which date from the time of the National Revival and the Anti-Turkish movement. Though it's true that the 19th-century atmosphere has been preserved, a large proportion of the buildings has suffered considerably.

SIGHTSEEING

A good place to start a tour of the city is at the end of Ulitsa Dimitar Blagoev, by the monument to the revolutionaries hanged on this spot in 1876.

ARCHEOLOGICHESKI MUZEJ (ARCHAEOLOGICAL MUSEUM)

The emphasis of the museum's collection is on the period from 1200 to 1400, when Veliko Tarnovo, after Pliska, Preslaw and Ohrid, was the fourth capital of the Bulgarian Empire. *Ulitsa Ivanka Boteva | Tue–Sun 8am–midday and 1–6.30pm*

ASENOVATA MAHALA (ASEN'S QUARTER)

All that remains of the medieval quarter, where craftsmen, merchants and minor clerics once used to live, are three churches. The oldest is *Sveti Dimitar Solunski* dating from 1185 on the northeastern slope of the Trapezica Hill. This was where, in 1185, the brothers Asen and Petar signalled the uprising against Byzantium. *Sveti Sveti Petar i Pavel* rises up directly opposite, on the other bank of the Jantra. The artistically most significant church is *Sveti 40 machenitsi* from the first half of the 13th century, and inside the columns of Khan Omurtag and Ivan Asen II are particularly worth seeing. The inscriptions on these columns are amongst the oldest pieces of writing still in existence which relate to medieval Bulgaria.

MUZEJ VAZRAZHDANE I UCHREDITELNO SABRANIE

The exhibits in the 'Museum of National Liberation and the Constituent Assembly' are evidence of the patriotic struggle of the Bulgarians against the Turks. One room which has remained unchanged is the room in which the first Bulgarian Parliament met and adopted the constitution in 1879. *Ploshtad Saedinenie | daily 10am–5pm*

STARIJA GRAD (OLD TOWN)

The best-known buildings in the Old Town are linked to Kolyu Ficheto, another name for the autodidact Nikola Fichev,

The remains of the Tsarevets Castle

who is regarded as the founder of modern architectural and national styles. The INSIDER TIP *Hadji Nikoli Tavern* *(Ulitsa Rakovski 17)* was built to his design as was the *House with the Monkey (Ulitsa Vastanicheska 14)*, a universally popular photo motif. The council building of the Turkish authorities, the *Konak (Ploshtad Saedinenie)*, where Bulgaria's first National Assembly accepted the constitution of the new state in 1879, was also designed by Fichev.

A row of stylish buildings is preserved on Ulitsa Gurko. The outstanding one is *Sarafkina House (Ulitsa Gurko 88 | Tue–Fri 9am–midday and 2–6pm)*, named after the money lender to whom it belonged, its magnificent interior design giving an insight into the taste and purchasing power of the wealthy Tarnovos family in the 19th century. The *Samovod-ska Chatshija* market area has been brought back to life with the arrival of small workshops where the master craftsmen go about their work.

TRAPEZITSA HILL

Nobles and high-ranking representatives of the clergy had their residences on this rather inaccessible hill. Some temporal buildings and the foundation walls of 17 medieval churches as well as parts of the decorations and murals have been unearthed.

TSAREVETS HILL ☆

The natural rock fortress on Tsarevets Hill formed the political and spiritual centre of the Second Bulgarian Empire. The foundations of the former *Tsarevets Castle* have been unearthed, and a part of the fortress walls, including *Baldwin's Tower*, has been restored. Whilst the excavations were being carried out, the foundations of residential and commercial buildings, churches and monasteries were also found.

On the top of the hill, where once the Patriarchal Cathedral – *Sveti Vaznesenie (Holy Ascension of God)* – stood, frescoes in the Socialist Realism style were painted on its remains in the 1980s. In the Middle Ages traitors were thrown down from the *Execution Rock* on the north summit *(Sightseeing 8am–7pm, winter 9am–5pm | guided tours tel. 062 63 49 46)*.

Bulgaria's history is symbolically represented in the enormous INSIDER TIP *Zvuk i svetlina son et lumière show*. The music was created for the show and the light effects make the past come alive. In inclement weather you can follow the show from an observation room by the Archaeological Museum. *Reservations and information tel. 062 63 69 52 or from the Tourist Information Centre.*

Once a year the fortress ruins are used as

the backdrop for a stage. At the start of August the **INSIDER TIP** *Szena na Veko vete* (Stage of the Centuries) Festival is held with opera and ballet performances. Tickets from the Tourist Information Centre or at the evening box office.

FOOD & DRINK

ETHNO

Restaurant serving Bulgarian, Arabian, Mexican and Italian cuisine. It serves specialities such as osso bucco (knuckle of veal) and *baba ganoush*, a starter made of aubergines, the recipe originating from the sultans' kitchen. *Bulevard Bulgaria 29 b | ethno-bg.com | Moderate*

INSIDER TIP **HAN HADJI NIKOLI**

This tavern is located in one of the city's finest 19th-century houses. It has been lavishly restored to its original state and won the national 'Building of the Year'

award in 2010. Han Hadji Nikoli is a gourmet and cultural centre boasting a unique atmosphere of comfort and authenticity with four restaurants, summer garden, wine bar, museum and art gallery. *Ulica Rakovski 19 | 062 65 12 91 | www.hanhad jinikoli.com | Moderate–Expensive*

WHERE TO STAY

HOTEL CENTRAL

Hotel in the Old Town near the river. Central location, private car park. *15 rooms | Ulitsa Hadzhi Dimitar 17 | tel. 062 60 60 96 | www.hotelcentral-bg.com | Budget*

HOTEL GURKO

Small, distinguished address in the Old Town, in a restored Revival building. The hotel restaurant serves traditional dishes. *21 rooms | Ulitsa Gurko 33 | tel. 062 62 78 38 | www.hotel-gurko.com | Budget– Moderate*

FAMOUS BULGARIANS

Cyril and Methodius, the inventors of the Slavic alphabet, have to be included in the list of Bulgaria's most famous Bulgarians. More recently, the installation artist Christo (born Christo Yavashev in Gabrovo in 1935) has made a name for himself, with his most celebrated project, such as the 'Wrapped Reichstag' in Berlin in 1995 providing spectacular and surprising perspectives. Bulgaria has also produced some famous singers. Veselina Katsarova is one of the most sought-after mezzo-sopranos in the world. The opera singers Boris Christoff and Nikolai Gyaurov were, during their lifetimes, considered the best bass singers in the world. The most fa-

mous Bulgarian tenor was Asparuh 'Ari' Leshnikov, founder member of the Berlin ensemble Comedian Harmonists. He went to Germany to study music in 1922, at the same time working as a waiter. He took the part of first tenor with the Comedian Harmonists. He returned to Bulgaria when the sextet broke up.
The Bulgarian national poet Ivan Vazov (1850–1921) is perhaps not well-known outside his native country. But the name Ilija Trojanov may be more familiar to English readers through his novel 'Along the Ganges'. He was born in Sofia in 1965 and has written several novels as well as non-fiction works and has received numerous awards for literature.

VELIKO TARNOVO TAVERN
A simple hotel, but from here it's only three minutes on foot to Tsarevets Hill. Other sights are also close by. *6 rooms | Ulitsa Chitalishtna 9 | tel. 062 62 11 62 | www.guesthouse-vt.com | Budget*

INFORMATION

TOURIST INFORMATION CENTRE
Ulitsa Hristo Botev 5 | tel. 062 62 21 48 | www.velikoturnovo.info

WHERE TO GO

ARBANASI ★ (127 D4) (∅ H4)
Although situated 4km/2.5mi northeast of Veliko Tarnovo, this village is regarded as one of the city's historic monuments and it also enjoys protected status. The houses built by prosperous merchants are surrounded by massive stone walls and equipped with ironwork gates and barred windows. This makes the buildings appear rather like well-fortified fortresses from the outside. But the interior design and furnishings give a quite different picture, with delicate woodcarvings on doors and ceilings, beautiful tiles and rich murals. Ten houses have been restored, two of them converted into museums, including *Dragostinov House*. The INSIDERTIP *Church of the Nativity of Christ* dating from the 17th century has a magnificent interior and is by far the most interesting of the five churches in Arbanasi. The wall paintings in the *Elias Chapel* of *Nikola Monastery* have the highest artistic worth of the cultural treasures on display in the two *monasteries – Sveti Nikola* and *Sveta Bogorodica*. The best view over the valley to the peaks of the Balkans is from the ✲ *Arbanasi Palace* Hotel, the former residence of Bulgaria's Communist ruler, Todor Zhivkov.

INSIDERTIP BOZHENTSI (126 C5) (∅ G4)
The museum village of Bozhentsi nestles in idyllic tranquillity a good 15km/9mi southeast of Gabrovo. Time seems to have stood still in the narrow streets, with ivy growing up and around the white-washed houses and over their stone-plate roofs. In the village centre there are wells and taverns just like 150 years ago. More than 100 buildings enjoy Unesco protected status and present an image, captured in time, of the Revival period.
The must-see building is the house of a rich wool trader dating from the early 19th century, *Kastata na Doncho Popa*. If you'd like to see how a peasant's home of this period was furnished, then seek out *Baba Kostadinica* house. If you are looking for a meal and a place to stay in the countryside, try *Kashta Mehana Dvata Shtrausa | 5 rooms | tel. 067193 3 84 | www.scraft.net/twoos | Budget*

ETARA ★ (126 C5–6) (∅ G4)
You will find the most original and picturesque open-air museum in Bulgaria a good 50km/31mi south of Veliko Tarnovo beyond Gabrovo. Standing alone in a forested area, its workshops are faithful copies of the originals and there are demonstrations of 26 traditional manual crafts. Visitors can stroll through the narrow streets and watch the artisans at work, practising regional crafts such as woodcarving, pottery, fulling, cutlery making and braid weaving, and their tools, equipment, machines and methods will be almost exactly the same as they were in this area at the time of the National Revival. There are also courses for handicraft enthusiasts. INSIDERTIP *Old Bulgarian customs* are celebrated with music and dance at Easter, Christmas and on the important Bulgarian saints days. You

Traditional crafts have been revived in the museum village of Etara

can also buy the finished articles here — they are of high quality and represent good value for money.

The museum village was founded by a private individual, becoming a state open air museum in 1963. Etara is easily accessible for tourists; on the site itself there is a wine bar serving Bulgarian dishes and a bakery right next door selling the area's popular white bread. There are several cafés where you can try the typical Bulgarian *bjalo sladko* ('white sweetness'), a mixture of sugar, water and spices.

Information is available at *www.etar.org* or in the *Stranopriemnica Hotel* which is part of the site*(39 rooms | tel. 066 810580 | Budget)*.

SHIPKA (126 C6) (*[map] G5*)

You can reach the *Shipchenski prohod* mountain pass via Gabrovo. This is a pass which, from a historical perspective, has so much significance for Bulgarians, for it was here in August 1877 that 6000 Rus-

sians and Bulgarians held out against massively superior Turkish forces for three days. If you climb the steps (there are very nearly 900 of them!) to the platform on the [symbol] memorial for the fallen Bulgarians and Russians, you'll be rewarded with a wonderful view of Rose Valley and the Sredna Gora Mountains.

TRYAVNA (126 C5) (*[map] G4*)

It's worth a detour to Tryavna (pop. 12,000), 40km/25mi southwest of Veliko Tarnovo, which features in Noah Gordon's bestselling novel 'The Physician' as a lively commercial centre. In the old part look out for interesting architecture from the 19th century and especially examples of Tryavna's famous painting and wood-carving school. In the *Daskalov House* two masters once had a wager as to who could carve the more beautiful ceiling. Six months later two wonderful examples, both with the sun in the middle, were completed. It is also famous for its textile industry.

NORTHEASTERN BULGARIA

The northeast of the country lies somewhat off the main tourist trail, but nonetheless it does have scenic charms of its own.

The Jantra and Beli Lom valleys break up the Danube table between Veliko Tarnovo and Ruse into smaller units, and further to the east there are wide areas of grass and scrubland, home only to flocks of sheep and herds of goats. This is also the location of the two centres of the first Bulgarian Empire in the Middle Ages: the first capital city Pliska which was destroyed and the subsequent capital Preslav. In the northeast it's mainly the Turkish minority which is represented in the centres of Razgrad and Shumen although, since 1878, the Bulgarians have left little of the Turkish architecture intact. The dominant features are the Danube and the city of Ruse, the main centre of the northeast. The location of this city on the Danube, a mighty river extending deep into the central Europe, does, however, offer opportunities for a brighter future.

RUSE

(127 D2) *(∅ H1)* ★ **In terms of its atmosphere and tradition, the city of Ruse (pop. 150,000) (with a voiceless ‚s' and final ‚e' sounded, pronounced ‚roo-seh'; the spellings 'Rousse' and 'Russe' are also found) is the most open of Bulgaria's major cities.**

Ruse was for a long time the 'gateway to the world', with its port opening up cen-

The Danube flows through a pastoral region often described as Bulgaria's 'Gateway to the World'

tral Europe. It was from here that the itinerant traders came on their way to Constantinople, bringing with them guest performances by foreign orchestras and introducing new music and instruments. Many famous people such as Emperor Franz Joseph, Empress Eugénie, Hans Christian Andersen and Franz Liszt raised the city's profile. Bulgaria's first railway line was built between Ruse and Varna in 1866. The economic and cultural boom was mainly due to the multi-ethnic community which developed here, with

WHERE TO START?

Ploshtad na svobodata: Start your tour of the city in Ruse at *Ploshtad na svobodata*, Freedom Square, which you can reach by buses 16 and 20 and trolley buses 25, 26, 27 and 29. Cars can be parked in the side streets. The inner city is small and it's easy to find your way around.

Central European architecture in Ruse

many Greeks, Armenians, some Germans and, the most numerous, Sephardic Jews. The Nobel Prize-winning writer Elias Canetti was born here in 1905 and spent the first years of his life in the city.

The city's appearance underlines its cosmopolitan character, the architecture pointing to the influence of many European styles with Baroque, Renaissance, Empire and Art Nouveau dominating the façades. There are also parks and boulevards, where you can enjoy a relaxing stroll.

SIGHTSEEING

ISTORICHESKI MUZEJ (HISTORICAL MUSEUM)

Silver treasures from the village of Borovo, Thracian craftwork and tools from the Bronze and Stone Age are displayed in the former castle *Dvorets Batenberg*; there's also an interesting ethnographic department. *Ploshtad Aleksandar Batenberg 3 | daily 9am–6pm*

MUZEJ NA TRANSPORTA I SAOBSHT-ENIJATA (NATIONAL TRANSPORT MUSEUM)

Bulgaria's very first train set off from the railway station here, travelling along the line connecting Ruse with the Black Sea city of Varna. The exhibits themselves, including old locomotive and carriages, stand on the railway tracks. The steam engine and saloon car belonging to Sultan Abdul Azis that date from 1866 are here, as well as the carriages used by Tsar Boris III and the Soviet Marshall Tolbuhin. *Ulitsa Bratja Obretenovi 13 | daily 8am–midday and 2–5.30pm*

SVETA TROITSA (CHURCH OF THE HOLY TRINITY)

This is the only Christian church (1632) of any great significance and, like many other Bulgarian churches, it was built half into the ground to avoid being too conspicuous. It houses a collection of ancient icons. *Ulitsa Goradhd 1*

FOOD & DRINK

BALKANSKA PRINZESA

The 'Balkan Princess' is a ship with a restaurant and cocktail bar on board; in the evening if the weather is fine, from 7.30pm it will also cruise the Danube. It serves traditional Bulgarian food with plenty of fish. *Port | Ulitsa Ponton 7 | Budget–Moderate*

MEHANA CHIFLIKA

The best traditional Bulgarian food in Ruse with some quite unusual casserole dishes on offer, in a rustic setting. *Ulitsa Otec Paisij 2 | Moderate*

DANUBE TRIPS

You can book day trips on the Rozhen cruise vessel to Svishtov or Tutrakan. Scenically, the excursion to Silistra is delightful, with a return journey taking two days. *Balgarsko rechno plavane | Ulitsa Otec Paisij 2 | tel. 082 83 37 77 | www.brp.bg* or *Dunav Tours | Ulitsa Olimpi Panov 5 | tel. 082 83 37 77 | www.dunavtours.bg*

ENTERTAINMENT

The city's philharmonic orchestra and the opera both enjoy a good reputation. The classical music festival *Martenski musikalni dni (www.roussefestival.mlnk.net)* is held in March. In addition to the *Sava Ognjanov Drama Theatre (Ploshtad na svoboda)*, where plays by Canetti are performed, Ruse also has a *Puppet Theatre.*

WHERE TO STAY

BEST WESTERN BISTRA I GALINA

This elegant hotel and multiple-award winner in the city centre has imaginative architecture, high comfort levels and a spa. *27 rooms, 2 apartments | Ulitsa Han Asparuch 8 | tel. 082 82 33 44 and tel. 082 23 43 71 | www.bghotel.bg | Moderate*

HOTEL RIGA

The largest hotel in the city is situated right on the banks of the Danube. The 16-storey building was conceived with the emphasis on functionality. The hotel has three restaurants, the best one being the ☆ *Panorama* which boasts superb cuisine and a splendid view of the Danube. *160 rooms, 9 apartments | Bulevard Pridunavski 22 | tel. 082 82 20 42 | www.hotel-riga.com | Moderate*

INFORMATION

TOURIST INFORMATION CENTRE

Ulitsa Aleksandrovska 61 | tel. 082 82 47 04 | www.tic.rousse.bg

WHERE TO GO

CHERVEN ARCHAEOLOGICAL RESERVE

(127 D3) (Ω J2)

Situated on a hill and surrounded by the river, this archaeological reserve with re-

---

MARCO POLO HIGHLIGHTS

mains of the medieval town of **INSIDER TIP Cherven** is situated 32km/20mi south of Ruse, in the Rusenski Lom Valley. The Thracians had a settlement here, which was extended in the 4th century into a fortress. During the reign of Tsar Ivan Asen II in the 13th century, the town was an important political, economic and cultural centre. Its walls which reach to a height of 5m have been preserved, as has one tower. Archaeologists have found the remains of 13 churches, built in the style of the Veliko Tarnovo school of architecture. *Cherven village | daily 8am–5pm*

RUSENSKI LOM NATURE PARK ⏱
(127 D–E 2–3) *(ᗰ J2)*

The Nature Park is situated in the canyon of the River Rusenski Lom, 20km/12mi southeast of Ruse. It's home to 174 species of birds and many animal species such as bats, foxes, wolves and red deer. The conditions in the park are particularly favourable to rock-nesting birds,

Wall paintings in the Rock-Hewn Churches of Ivanovo

such as the golden eagle. There are also 870 types of plants here. The park administration offices are in Ruse *(Bulevard Skobelev 7 | tel. 082 87 23 97).*

Bulgaria's only cave monastery still occupied by monks, the **INSIDER TIP Sveti Dimitar Besarabovski** is situated in the Rusenski Lom valley. *By the village of Besarabovo, 10km/6mi south of Ruse*

SKALNI CHERKVI PRI IVANOVO (ROCK-HEWN CHURCHES OF IVANOVO) ★ (127 D2) *(ᗰ H2)*

The rocks, located 22km/14mi south of Ruse and which rise up 32m above the Rusenski Lom, are home to some of the few remaining examples of medieval Bulgarian art, and these wall paintings from the Tarnovo school in the cave monastery are under Unesco protection. Settlers established themselves here in the 12th century and began to build a monastery complex in the rocky gorges, the most famous part of which, a cave known as 'The Church', is thought to have been built between 1331 to 1371. *Daily 9am–6pm*

INSIDER TIP THRACIAN TOMB
(128 A3) *(ᗰ K2)*

This ancient monument built for a Thracian ruler dates from the first half of the 3rd century BC. It lies a good 80km/50mi to the east by Sveshtari (near Isperih) and consists of three chambers: an entrance chamber and two antechambers covered by a mound. Now a Unesco World Heritage Site, the architecture, murals and decorative work are truly remarkable.

SHUMEN

(128 A5) *(ᗰ K3)* **Shumen (pop. 100,000) is the perfect example of what happens to a city's appearance, when a new regime wishes to make its mark.**

As a result of the actions of Bulgaria's 'national liberators' from 1878, hardly any traces remain of the Ottoman period, apart from the Tombul Mosque. The socialists' attempts to urbanise the heart of the city are also clearly evident, with numerous grand buildings now lining the main street. Nonetheless, the city is worth a visit and in addition to the Tombul Mosque, there are a few interesting

a fine view of Shumen. *Steps from Bulevard Slavjanski, follow the signs southwards through the park*

TOMBUL DZHAMIJA (TOMBUL MOSQUE) ★

The largest preserved mosque from the Ottoman period, the Tombul Mosque was erected by Sherif Halil Pascha in 1744, with columns from the castle of the

Tombul Mosque – largest preserved testament to Ottoman culture in Bulgaria

examples of 19th-century architecture to look out for. The city is also the starting point for excursions to Preslav and Pliska, as well as to the Madara Horseman relief. The Madara caves, once used by Thracians as sites of worship, are places for quiet relaxation.

SIGHTSEEING

'1300 YEARS OF BULGARIA' ☽

This concrete monument presents Bulgaria's past as a mosaic, the nation's history chiselled into the rock, and it offers

first Bulgarian tsar in Pliska being incorporated into the building. The courtyard of the Koran school is dominated by a well house. Used as a museum during the socialist era, the mosque is today once more a house of prayer. There's a fine view from the ☽ clock tower – its bell has sounded the hour every hour without interruption since 1740. *Ulitsa Rakovski 21 | daily 9am–6pm*

REVIVAL ARCHITECTURE

The greatest concentration of houses from the 19th century can be seen around

Ulitsa Tsar Osvoboditel, which runs through the heart of the old town. Near the mosque stands the splendid *Djukmedzhjan House (Ulitsa Stara planina 14)*, built in the middle of the 19th century. Lajos Kossuth, the leader of the 1848 Hungarian Revolution lived in the *Kossuth House (Ulitsa Tsar Osvoboditel 35 | Mon–Fri 9am–5pm)* for a few months. The *Pancho Vladigerov House (Ulitsa Tsar Osvoboditel 136 | Mon–Fri 9am–5pm)* not only documents the life and work of Bulgaria's patriarch of classical music, but also shows the typical interior furnishings of a dwelling at the beginning of the 20th century. Concerts are held in the chamber music room and in the garden, and every year there's a competition for young pianists and violinists.

FOOD & DRINK

MEHANA CHIFLIKA
This is a traditionally furnished restaurant with two dining rooms and summer garden. It offers Bulgarian cuisine, with dishes of grilled pork and lamb as specialities, served on a sach (clay dish). At the foot of the Ilchov Hill in the city centre. *Ulitsa Bladaisko vastanie 181 | www.mehanachiflika.com | Moderate*

POPSHEITANOVA KASHTA
This is a tavern with rustic-style furnishings in a lovely building dating from the 18th–19th century, serving local specialities. There's a summer garden for fine weather. *Ulitsa Tsar Osvoboditel 158 | www.popsheytanova.com | Budget–Moderate*

WHERE TO STAY

ART HOTEL NIRVANA
Situated at the foot of the hill with the 'Monument to 1300 Years of Bulgaria', the hotel boasts an eastern architectural style and rooms in various colours, which are said to symbolise the body's chakras (energy centres). It has a Turkish bath, outdoor swimming pool, restaurant and café. *7 rooms, 1 apartment | Ulitsa Nezavisimost 25 | tel. 054 80 01 27 | www.hotelnirvana.bg | Budget*

HOTEL MINALIAT VEK (THE LAST CENTURY)
Listed building, lavishly renovated and faithful to the original, with the atmosphere of a middle class house at the start of the 20th century. *7 rooms, 2 apartments | Bulevard Simeon Veliki 81 | tel. 054 80 16 15 | www.minaliatvek.com | Budget*

HOTEL SOLO
The hotel enjoys a central location. The rooms are light but rather small. Ask about the room with a large terrace. *7 rooms | Ulitsa Panaiot Volov 2 | tel. 054 98 15 71 | www.hotelsolo-bg.com | Budget*

LOW BUDGET

▶ With a fashionable clientele and not too expensive, the *Happy Bar & Grill* restaurant serves tasty food and represents value for money. It's situated in Ruse's pedestrian zone. *Ploshtad na svobodata*

▶ The *Chiflik Elena (4 rooms)* hotel in the village of Kjulevcha offers self-catering accommodation. The hosts organise excursions, donkey safaris and folklore evenings with traditional food. Madara and Pliska are nearby. *Information Bulevard Slavyanski 48 in Shumen | tel. 054 5 74 30 | chiflikelena.com*

The Madara Horseman relief is a Unesco World Heritage Site

TOURIST INFORMATION CENTRE
Bulevard Slavjanska 17 | tel. 054 85 77 73 | www.shumen.bg

WHERE TO GO

SHUMEN FORTRESS (128 A5) *(ωK3)*
The fortress, 3km/2mi to the west, is 3200 years old and was destroyed in the 15th century. Archaeological excavations are being carried out here. Open air museum. *Daily 9am–5pm*

MADARA ★ (128 B5) *(ωL3)*
This famous monumental relief from the 8th century is regarded as one of the most important testaments to Bulgaria's cultural history. It is situated on a cliff some 100m high, below the old Madara Fortress, approx. 15km/9mi east of Shumen. Chiselled into the cliff wall at a height of 23m, the relief shows a horseman thrusting his lance into a prostrate lion, with a dog running at his side. The inscriptions are the oldest known sources of the word 'Bulgaria'. *Daily 9am–5pm*

PLISKA (128 B4–5) *(ωL3)*
Today, only a few ruins remain of Pliska (25km/15mi northeast), which was until 893 the capital of the first Bulgarian Empire. The adjacent museum is providing help in the reconstruction. *Site and museum daily 9am–5pm | tel. 05323 20 12*

VELIKI PRESLAV (128 A5) *(ωK3)*
The striking remains of the former capital of the first Bulgarian Empire (10th century) are situated 20km/12mi southwest of Shumen. The town, which dates back to a Slav settlement, was previously surrounded by two fortress walls: the inner wall, the citadel, and the outer which was meant to protect the whole area of the town. One part of the wall is preserved, as are remains of the north and south gates, the palace, the monasteries and some workshops. Beyond the south gate stands the *Golden Church* which is worth seeing, its interior decorated with a mosaic. In the archaeological park *Museum,* displays include an exhibition of beautiful ceramics. *Site and museum daily 8am–5pm | www.museum-preslav. com*

BLACK SEA COAST

The Black Sea coast is the best-known and most popular area in Bulgaria. Nature has bestowed the 378-km (235-mi) coastline with a wealth of pristine beaches and beautiful scenery.

The Bulgarians divide the Black Sea coast into two sections: the north with Varna as its centre and the south with Burgas at its heart. The division also has something to do with a split into two almost ideological factions. Many Sofians adamantly swear that the beaches in the south are much more beautiful, a statement which residents of Varna in turn consider typical of the spiteful remarks people from the major cities make about them.

But it has to be said that both parts have their own particular charm. The north is so attractive with its wonderful rocky landscapes around Balchik and especially near Kaliakra where reddish rocks rise up out of the sea to a height of 60 to 70m. In addition, the north is a winner with its golden beaches, and in Varna it almost certainly possesses the more interesting major city.

In the south, however, the sand is visibly lighter and finer. Around Primorsko where the Ropotamo flows into the sea, the luxuriant vegetation and the creepers entwined in the trees create a subtropical ambience. The small picturesque towns of Nessebar and Sozopol adorn this section of the coast.

Photo: Balchik Castle

A charming contrast – bleak rocky landscapes in the north and small picturesque towns in the south

BURGAS

(135 D–E3) (*∅ M5*) **Burgas (pop. 230,000) is an industrial city and the economic, administrative and cultural centre of Bulgaria's southern Black Sea coast.**
The largest crude oil refinery on the Balkan peninsula is located a few kilometres to the north and the city boasts the biggest port in the country and also one of the busiest airports. It's also the centre of the Bulgarian fishing and fish processing

industry. So you see for most tourists Burgas is only a stepping stone to the southern Black Sea coast. But there's a pedestrian zone with cafés and restaurants, plus the inevitable souvenir shops.

SIGHTSEEING

The most important sights are concentrated in the city centre around *Aleksandrovska* and *Aleko Bogoridi streets*. Worthy of mention are the *Archaeological Museum (Bogoridi 21)*, the *Sveti Sveti Kiril i Me-*

A gentle stroll in the small town of Nessebar

todij *Cathedral* and the small *Armenian Church* in *Ulitsa General Major Lermontov.*

FOOD & DRINK

RESTAURANT GROLSCH
This traditional restaurant serves fish, sea food and steak specialities. *Primorski Park (in the Sea Garden by the Flora Café) | Budget*

RESTAURANT POD LIPITE (UNDER THE LINDEN TREES)
The buildings were once the meeting place for Bulgarian merchants. In the restaurant you can enjoy fine, traditional Bulgarian food and there is also a summer garden. *Ulitsa Al. Batenberg 14 | Moderate–Expensive*

ENTERTAINMENT

Burgas has its own Philharmonic Orchestra, theatre and opera house with performances in the Sea Garden during the summer. In the middle of August the Rock and Pop Festival 'Spirit of Burgas' is held on the central beach. The Folklore Festival at the end of August is another highlight. The in place to meet is the *Addict* club *(Ulitsa Vazrazhdane 6).*

WHERE TO STAY

HOTEL BULGARIA
This hotel enjoys a central location in a large functional building. *163 rooms, 8 apartments | Ulitsa Aleksandrovska 21 | tel. 056 84 26 10 and 056 84 28 20 | www. bulgaria-hotel.com | Expensive*

BURGAS PLAZA
Beautifully furnished, this is a small hotel offering many luxuries. *11 rooms, 5 apartments | Bulevard Bogoridi 42 | tel. 056 84 62 94 | www.plazahotel-bg.com | Expensive*

INFORMATION

TOURIST INFORMATION CENTRE
Ulitsa Hristo Botev, pedestrian subway by the theatre | tel. 056 82 57 72 | www.tic. burgas.bg.

There are also tourist services in the foyer of the Bulgaria Hotel.

WHERE TO GO

KITEN, LOZENEC, AHTOPOL AND SINE-MORETS (135 F5) (*M6*)

The further south you go, the higher the temperatures, the hotter the sand and the more INSIDERTIP▶ unspoilt the surroundings. This makes a trip to Kiten, Lozenec, Ahtopol and Sinemorets worthwhile. The south offers campers great opportunities to pitch their tents far away from the busy spots. There are good bus connections to the nearest larger towns.

INSIDERTIP▶ ROPOTAMO NATURE RESERVE (135 E4) (*M6*)

About 10km/6mi south of Sozopol you come to a swampy, forested area where a brief stop and a short boat trip are essential. The Ropotamo Nature Reserve *(Naroden Park)*, once the exclusive hunting grounds belonging to Communist Party leader Todor Zhivkov, is today, at least in high summer, an almost tropical paradise of graceful flora and fauna. As soon as there are ten interested people, the waiting cruise boats set off. It's clearly signposted from the road.

NESSEBAR ★ (135 E3) (*M5*)

Situated on a rocky peninsula 35km/22mi to the northeast, this small town is as pretty as a postcard. Its ancient origins are at once clearly evident from its restricted confines. Nessebar has numerous magnificent examples of medieval architecture and the centre's labyrinth of narrow streets is full of picturesque buildings in the Revival style. The resort (pop. 9000) is a delightful spot. As you approach you see the windmill to the left and behind it the remains of the ancient

town wall by the harbour. Waiting there is a unique collection of medieval church buildings, some carefully preserved. But it's the 19th-century architecture which creates the romantic atmosphere. Both the façade as well as the interior make *Lambrinov House* and even more so *Muskojani House* really worth seeing. In total 60 buildings from the so-called Revival period are preserved.

Nessebar, with its numerous hotels and restaurants, is well developed for tourists, but the commercialisation will soon reach its limits and, if you're travelling independently, you should really avoid making a visit in the high season.

If you'd like to enjoy a coffee together with a view from a rocky terrace by the sea, then you should drop in at the ☆ *Bistro Zornica (Budget)* near the old Metropolitan Church. Fish is served all over the peninsula; enjoy a quiet moment in the *Neptune restaurant (Budget)* or on one of the three terraces at the *Andromeda restaurant* in *Ulitsa Ivan Aleksandar 19 (Moderate)*. The ● *Chevermeto* restaurant right next to the seashore serves traditional Bulgarian cuisine and *cheverme*. In the summer the daredevil *Nestinari* fire dancers display their talents on glowing coals *(by the south beach | www.chevermeto-nessebar.com)*.

Information about events, excursions etc. at the *Tourist Information Centre (Ulitsa Mesembria 10 | tel. 0554 4 26 11 | www. visitnessebar.org)*.

SLANCHEV BRYAG (SUNNY BEACH)
(135 E2) (∅ M5)

Sunny Beach, 35km/22mi north of Burgas, is the biggest holiday complex in the country. By the 8-km (5-mi) long, crescent-shaped beach there are over 100 hotels, more than 130 bars, medical centres, open air theatres, sports venues and shops. The holiday complex has always consciously sought to present itself as children and family friendly, but it suffers from the usual weaknesses of a tourist enclave. Especially in recent years Sunny Beach has become a negative example of uncontrolled building frenzy. Most of the hotel and residential buildings stand empty or are only half finished

In the summer the water temperature on the Black Sea coast is a perfect 22°C/72°F

because foreign investors and buyers failed to show up.

SOZOPOL (135 E4) (*M5*) ●

Situated on a rocky peninsula 30km/20mi southeast of Burgas, the ★ *Old Town* of Sozopol (pop. 5000) contains an abundance of attractive buildings dating from the 19th century. Cypresses line the narrow cobbled streets; fishing nets and, beneath the eaves, fish are left to dry in the sun.

The church most worth a visit is *Sveta Bogorodica* with its icons and woodcarvings. The *Archaeological Museum* houses a remarkable collection of Greek vases. The finest houses, cafés and restaurants are to be found in the area round *Ulitsa Apolonija* and *Kiril i Metodij and the b*est places to eat and drink are the *Mehana Vjatarna Melnica (Ulitsa Morski Skali |*

Moderate), which you'll find if you walk straight on through the town (easily recognisable by the small windmill), and the *Mehana Ksantana (Moderate)*. Both places serve fish dishes and national specialities. The *Kirik* restaurant *(Ulitsa Ribarska 77)* INSIDER TIP serves fish in a garlic sauce based on their own recipe.

VARNA

(129 D5) (*N3*) ★ **Its enchanting location is the major asset of the city (pop. 350,000), and the people of Varna have made the most of it.**

In addition to the beaches (north, central, south) a wonderful, huge Sea Garden was laid out in 1878 and it is still an inviting place to take a relaxing stroll. The Old Town of Varna – where Greeks founded Odyssos in 570 BC – is not exactly in tip-top condition and it exudes the homely atmosphere of a settlement which has grown too fast. A travel guide from the 1920s described the coastal town as the 'most restorative sea spa in south-eastern Europe'. The bathing area with changing rooms from this time has been preserved, but today the area is mainly occupied by restaurants, bars, clubs and discos. Thousands of people

> **WHERE TO START?**
> At the junction of Bulevard **Knjaz Boris and Bulevard Slivnitsa** is where you should start your tour. Buses 8, 9 and 14 go to the starting point (bus stop Sevastopol). It's best to leave the car in Varna because parking in the centre can be very difficult, although you could try the *Cherno More* Hotel car park right next to the junction.

Try to fit in a visit to the Archaeological Museum in Varna

cavort around till the small hours along the 3-km (2-mi) long city promenade. Prices are moderate, a cocktail costing about 4 leva. The local beach is where the people of Varna usually like to meet up, away from all the tourists. Varna has lots to offer, including an outstanding festival of classical music, theatre, opera and ballet which attracts international stars. You can spend many a balmy summer's evening listening to beautiful sounds perhaps first of all in the festival complex, but there's also the lovely open-air theatre in the Sea Garden.

SIGHTSEEING

ARCHEOLOGICHESKI MUZEJ (ARCHAEOLOGICAL MUSEUM) ★
The highlights of the collection (50,000 exhibits from the pre-historic period to the Middle Ages) are the artefacts in a tomb dating from the Copper Age (5000–4000 BC). More than a third of the unearthed tombs from this time contained no skeletons, but only symbolic funerary items: lots of jewellery, objects made of pure gold, cylinder-shaped pearls, and also tools and vessels. The jewellery is said to be oldest worked gold ever to have been discovered. The museum also houses an exhibition of Bulgarian icons from the 16th to the19th century. *Bulevard Marija Luiza 41 | Tue–Sun (in winter Tue–Sat) 10am–5pm| www.amvarna.com*

ETNOGRAFSKI MUZEJ (ETHNOGRAPHIC MUSEUM)
A picture of everyday life at the turn of the 20th century is presented in one of the few restored buildings of the Revival period – traditional dress, handicraft and jewellery, scenes of traditional festivals and rituals, as well as the original furnishings from rooms of this era. *Ulitsa Panagjurishte 22 | Tue–Sun (in winter Mon–Fri) 10am–5pm*

MORSKA GRADINA (SEA GARDEN)

The Sea Garden starts at the harbour and stretches several kilometres along the coast. This huge park was laid out in 1878 and has been extended over the years. It contains some museums (Natural History Museum, Naval Museum), a planetarium, a dolphinarium, an aquarium and a zoo. There are restaurants and cafés, tennis courts and an open-air theatre in the park as well as a children's play area with pedalos, slides and other attractions for the little ones. The Sea Garden is a popular meeting place for residents of Varna, especially on hot summer days.

RIMSKI TERMI (ROMAN THERMAL BATHS) ★

Varna was part of the Roman Empire in the 2nd and 3rd century, and the mild climate and healing mineral springs attracted affluent Romans. The remains of the baths covering 2.5 acres in the southeast of the city provide an insight into Roman bathing culture. Some three quarters of the site is taken up by the thermal baths, and remains of the duct system, cisterns and numerous rooms and halls, some reaching up to an impressive height, have been unearthed. *Ulitsa San Stefano/corner of Han Krum | Tue–Sun (in winter Tue–Sat) 10am–5pm| 8 lv*

SVETO USPENIE BOGORODICHNO (CATHEDRAL OF THE ASSUMPTION OF THE BLESSED VIRGIN)

Varna's cathedral was built between 1884 and 1886. The iconostasis, the three-panelled picture wall which was created by Macedonian masters from Debar and installed in 1912, is definitely worth a look; the rich wall paintings date from 1949/50. *Ploshtad Mitropolit Simeon 8 | daily 7am–6pm*

FOOD & DRINK

LA FAMILIA

Offers a wide choice of Italian cuisine, all ingredients locally sourced. *Ulitsa Bregalnica 1 | Budget*

 MR. BABA

This restaurant is a replica of 15th-century galleon. Guests can sit inside as well as up on deck, right next to the beach alongside the large Varna breakwater. The restaurant serves fish, sea food and other dishes and has a specialist wine waiter. A reservation is recommended. *By the south beach | tel. 052 61 46 29 | Expensive*

LOW BUDGET

▶ It's not as flexible as a hire car, but on the other hand it's much cheaper: tourists and locals use the minibus to get to practically every place, no matter how small, on the Black Sea coast and in the surrounding area. There are several buses every day. Tickets purchased on the bus or at the bus station: *Minibus Avtogara (Minibus Station) in Varna | Ulitsa Dobrovoltsi 7 (opposite bus station) | tel. 052 50 00 39 and 052 44 83 49 | www.minibus-varna.com or Avtogara Burgas, next to the railway station*

▶ Detours to Balchik, Pomorie or Tsarevo are well worth the effort, because, once you get away from the main tourist centres, prices in restaurants, the fruit and vegetable markets and the food shops are considerably lower than in Slanchev Bryag, Zlatni Pyasatsi or Albena.

PETTE KJOSHETA (THE FIVE CORNERS)
This small, cosy *mehana* serves tradi-tional Bulgarian cuisine using its own recipes. *Ulitsa Graf Ignatiev 29.* There's a second *mehana: Pette kjosheta 2 | Ulitsa Tsarevets 38 | Moderate*

SHOPPING

The pedestrian zone sells everything you could possibly desire. In *Ulitsa Knjaz Boris I you'll* find trinkets, souvenirs and now and again a good pair of shoes or some-thing fashionable to wear.

ENTERTAINMENT

From the middle of June to the middle of August, there are almost daily concerts, performances of opera or ballet by en-sembles from all over the world. *X-trava-ganca is a* trendy disco by *Ribarskija Plazh* beach *(Ulitsa Krajbrezhnaja Aleja).*

WHERE TO STAY

The numerous travel agents in the city will arrange hotels and private accom-modation.

CHERNO MORE BLACK SEA CASINO HOTEL
The largest and also most comfortable hotel in Varna is situated right in the cen-tre near the Morska Gradina (Sea Gar-den). From the �·ᴸ panoramic restaurant you can enjoy a INSIDER TIP ▶ wonderful view of the city. *200 rooms | Bulevard Slivnica 33 | tel. 052 612243 | www.cher nomorebg.com | Moderate–Expensive*

CITIUS HOTEL
This is a comfortable hotel in the centre of Varna, within walking distance of all the sights. The hotel offers a complimen-tary shuttle service to and from the air-port. Take breakfast in the neighbouring café. *25 rooms | Ulitsa Baba Rada 6 | tel. 052 62 23 32 | www.hotelvarna.bg | Budget*

VILLA DUCHESS
This modern hotel is housed in an old villa in the Sea Garden. The building is owned by the Dutch Bulgarian Cultural Centre. *8 rooms | Ulitsa Saltanat 64 | tel. 052 71 66 44 | www.duchess.nl | Moderate*

INFORMATION

BG TOURS VARNA
Ulitsa Bdin 25 | tel. 052 60 14 48 and 052 61 21 44 | www.bgtoursvarna.com
Further information at: *www.columbus-tour.com*

WHERE TO GO

EVKSINOGRAD (129 D5) (*ⓜ N3*)
Evksinograd Castle, the summer resi-dence of the tsars, is situated on the eastern edge of Varna, one exit before Sveti Sveti Konstantin i Elena. Prince Al-exander von Battenberg convalesced here and Tsar Boris III used the estate as a summer residence. Todor Zhivkov, lead-er of the Communist Party, also stayed here, but chose to sleep in the so-called summer bungalow. Today the site is still a hotel owned by the government and is therefore only rarely open to the public. But it's worth a visit if only for the lovely parklands.

POBITI KAMANI (STONE FOREST) (129 D5) (*ⓜ M3*)
It's not really known how these most unusual stone columns 20km/12mi to the west were formed. Some rise to a height of 6m and the size of their foun-dations differs considerably. They look like dripstone formations, the difference

being that they're on the surface. Experts estimate they are 50 million years old. *On the road to Sofia, direction Devnja*

SVETI SVETI KONSTANTIN I ELENA

(129 D5) *(N3)*
Hidden in a secluded spot between Varna and Golden Sands, this is actually the oldest spa in Bulgaria, although it is not very well-known. Bask in the sun on the beach in one of the several small sheltered bays. Life goes on here at a rather leisurely pace, but that doesn't mean you have to go without evening entertainment. There are numerous restaurants and cafés on the central shopping avenue. There is a large, wooded spa park, an inviting spot for an evening stroll. *Sveti Konstantin* monastery dates from the 15th century and gave the place its name.
Towering over all the other hotels (literally!), the *Grand Hotel Varna (235 rooms | tel. 052 361089 | www.gh-varna.com | Expensive)* boasts an equally outstanding restaurant, but be warned, it is rather expensive. The INSIDER TIP *Panorama on the twelfth floor* of the International Home of Scientists in the Frederik J. Curie Hotel complex is a pleasant café serving nice cakes and offering a lovely view.

A natural curiosity– the Stone Forest with bizarre stone columns

ZLATNI PYASATSI (GOLDEN SANDS)

(129 E5) *(M3)* **This unspoilt holiday resort north of Varna is the most successful resort on the Black Sea.**
Golden Sands is all the more remarkable because of the attractive juxtaposition of peaceful beach and wooded hillsides which slope down in terraces

to the sea. The setting creates a sheltered atmosphere within the site. The 3.5km/2mi long beach is in parts 100m wide and is covered in fine golden shimmering sand. In addition to the hotels there are countless restaurants, discos, bars and shops. Miniature tourist trains provide a regular service in the seaside resort, stopping at all the important destinations. The beach season lasts from the middle of May to the middle of October. In spring the colder weather lasts for a little longer, but in autumn the weather often stays mild until later.

FOOD & DRINK

Golden Sands has an outstanding range of restaurants, cafés and cars. The *Kosharata* and *Ciganski tabor (both Budget– Moderate)* serve good grilled food accompanied by gypsy music and folk dancing.

CHANOVETE
Roasted lamb is a speciality of this restaurant on the beach promenade in the southern part of the complex. *Moderate– Expensive*

INSIDER TIP ▶ RIVIERA
The fish restaurant is also called *Ribkata* (the little fish). It's situated right on the beach and serves freshly caught fish and an outstanding fish soup. *On the Riviera Holiday Club site | Moderate–Expensive*

SPORTS & ACTIVITIES

Equipment for sailing, surfing, waterskiing and parasailing can be hired from various places, for example the yacht club on the central beach. Lots of hotels have indoor and/or open-air pools and tennis courts, such as the *Prima Sol Sunlight* and *Berlin Green Park.* Golden Sands and the surrounding area can be explored on several cycle trails. Bikes and rickshaw hire in numerous places.

Lively night-life at Golden Sands

ENTERTAINMENT

There are lots of great places to spend an evening, but *Papaya* and *Astera* are very popular discos.

WHERE TO STAY

If you're travelling alone, it can be difficult to find a room in the summer.

HOTEL IMPERIAL

An awkward looking building, but equipped with everything that matters. François Mitterrand and Erich Honecker, amongst others, have stayed here in the Presidential Suite. It has a lovely ☀ *café* with a view of the sea. *46 rooms, 28 apartments | tel. 052 38 67 07 | www.riviera bulgaria.com | Expensive*

HOTEL PERUNIKA

Rather more basic and cheaper, but with its own pool. *163 rooms | tel. 052 35 53 10 | www.perunika.com | Moderate*

INFORMATION

Tourist information is available in the individual hotels as well as in the travel agents in Varna. *www.goldensands.bg*

WHERE TO GO

ALADZHA MANASTIR (ALADZHA CAVE MONASTERY) (129 D5) (*ω N3*)

A cave monastery dating from the 13th or 14th century, two storeys have been hollowed out in the limestone cliffs which were once connected by steps. There's a lovely view from the ☀ limestone cliffs, including a delightful panorama of the Black Sea. Above Golden Sands, take a walk through the trees past wooden benches and small springs. *Summer daily 9am–6pm, winter Tue–Sun 9am–4pm*

ALBENA (129 E4) (*ω N3*)

10km/6mi north with more than 50 hotels, three campsites and a 7-km (4-mi) long beach, up to 100m wide. There are countless sports venues, shops, facilities for children and bars. Albena is situated right next to the ☺ *Baltata Nature Reserve* covering an area of some 450 acres. The wood, though not easily accessible, is home to a wide range of flora and fauna and on the edge there are some observation points, for example at the Gergana Hotel. There's a nudist beach to the south of Albena in the direction of Kranevo. *www.albena.bg*

The INSIDER TIP ▶ *Chiflika Chukurovo* complex with the atmosphere of an old Bulgarian manor is situated 20km/12mi to the west of Albena in the village of Prilep **(129 D4)** (*ω N3*) There's a traditional restaurant here serving excellent food. Enormous menu, hotel accommodation, plus swimming pool, wine bar, museum and stables. *www.bulgarianecotravel.net*

ZLATNI PYASATSI (GOLDEN SANDS)

BALCHIK ✲ (129 E4) *(Ⓜ N3)*
White limestone cliffs extend through the town and along the coast. The one place worth visiting is the Dvoreca *Estate* (daily 9am–8pm) with the castle of the Romanian Queen Maria and the park containing a botanical garden and a large collection of cacti. You can watch Christian Orthodox weddings in the INSIDER TIP *Lovers' Alley*. There are two restaurants on the site. Join in a wine tasting at the ● *Gostnata na kralitsata* (Queen's living room) and admire some pieces of furniture which once belonged to Queen Maria. With a ✲ summer terrace. *www.balchik.com*.

Take a ● boat trip from the harbour in Balchik along the bay on the 'Aurora' accompanied by skipper Miro. Ask for him at the harbour.

INSIDER TIP **LAKE DURANKULAK** ●
(129 F3) *(Ⓜ O2)*
The last few kilometres before the Bulgarian-Romanian border form a natural paradise with white beaches and an unspoilt steppe landscape. This is where Lake Durankulak is situated, with just a narrow strip of sand separating it from the Black Sea. The calm water is an important natural habitat and home to 260 species of flora and fauna as well as a

BOOKS & FILMS

▶ **Under the Yoke** – Ivan Vazov, the author of this novel, was born in Sopot in Rose Valley and is often referred to as the 'patriarch of Bulgarian literature'. It was first published in 1893 and has been translated into over 30 languages. It tells of the bloody uprising of 1876 when Bulgarian patriots fought to throw off 500 years of Ottoman oppression, and is filled with action, romance, tragedy and humour. It was made into a film by Dako Dakovski in 1952.

▶ **Mission London** – In Bulgaria the fact that lots of things are different, but not everything's wrong is a theme that Alek Popov takes up in his first novel. It has been widely acclaimed as 'the funniest contemporary Bulgarian book' for its satirical portrayal of the Bulgarian elite. It was made into a film in 2010 by Dimitar Mitovski and attracted record numbers into cinemas, outselling Avatar!

▶ **Time of Parting** – The novel by Anton Donchev tells a story from the 17th century when Bulgaria was part of the Ottoman Empire. It's been translated into 30 languages and was filmed in 1988 with the title ‚Vreme na nasilie' (Time of Violence). The work by the director Ljudmil Staikov, considered by many to be the best Bulgarian film of all time, was filmed in the village of Kovachevitsa and it is available on DVD in Bulgarian with English subtitles.

▶ **Natural Novel** – Georgi Gospodinov's first novel is both broad in scope and intensely personal, illustrating the impossibility of presenting life truthfully. It contains a wealth of different story lines, reflections and digressions and an attempt to write a book using only verbs! But even more impressive than the academic gymnastics are the author's candid and rarely glimpsed snapshots of life in post-communist Bulgaria.

major overwintering area for many birds. The remains of a 6000-year-old settlement on the large island can be reached on foot. You can arrange bird watching tours and accommodation (*Budget–Moderate*) at the information centre *Branta Birding Lodge (on the main road to the border | tel. 0888 47 66 01 | www.branta-tours.com).*

KAMEN BRJAG (BRYAG)
(129 F4) (*ØØ O2*)

Kamen Bryag or 'Stone Bank' is situated 18km/11mi east of Kavarna and 5km/3mi north of Cape Kaliakra on a ⋇ steep romantic coast. Bring some fish to barbecue because there's a ● free natural gas fire for all to use. And adjacent you'll find the INSIDER TIP *Jailata* Nature Reserve with an archaeological excavation site, 4000-year-old Thracian tombs, sacrificial altars and the remains of a fortress from the early Byzantine period (5th century). The caves in the steep cliff face were occupied in antiquity, but the remains of the cave town are only accessible in a few places, and even then with difficulty. Information is available at the entrance to the nature reserve *(Information centre with parking)* or in the *Historical Museum in Kavarna (Ulitsa Chernomorska 1b | tel. 0570 8 21 50).* Local residents offer guest rooms. In the village there's a small hotel with restaurant *(Trite kestena (Three Chestnuts) | 7 rooms | tel. 0570 4 27 59 | Budget)*

CAPE KALIAKRA ★ ⋇
(129 F4–5) (*ØØ O3*)

The cliffs rise up to 70m above the sea, providing a wonderful view of the ● sunset. In earlier times the cape was used for defence, the Thracians having built a fortress here. Remains of the fortress walls have been uncovered and partly, though rather clumsily, re-erected. The

Rocky coastline at Cape Kaliakra

Monument to the Dead Girls symbolises the suicide of 40 maidens. They jumped to their deaths rather than be handed over to the Ottoman forces.

The village of Balgarevo is situated on the way to the cape between Kavarna and Kaliakra. Some 300m before you reach it, there's a road leading to the Dalboka mussel farm: a simply furnished restaurant (Moderate) with a unique menu: INSIDER TIP mussels filled with rice, cheese or apples, mussel salad and soups.

TRIPS & TOURS

The tours are marked in green in the road atlas,
pull-out map and on the back cover

1

CENTRAL BULGARIA – THE BALKAN MOUNTAINS, ROSES AND HISTORY

This route combines three beautiful landscapes: the Balkans, Rose Valley and a view of the Sredna Gora central mountains. It takes you to sites relating to Bulgarian history which were of particular importance at the time of the National Revival and during the war of liberation against the Ottoman Empire.

It measures 150km/93mi in total and actual driving time is from two and a half to three hours. But because of all the sites, it's more sensible to plan for over two days and to break the tour overnight in Kazanlak.

Begin the trip with a walk round **Koprivshtitsa → p. 62**, an enchanting little town. From here it's 13km/8mi to Highway no. 6 which you join and turn right in the direction of Kazanlak and Burgas. You are now on the 'line at the foot of the Balkans' *(Podbalkanska Linija)* as it's known by the Bulgarians.

The next highlight starts at the summit of the Klisura Pass. From here to Kazanlak (just under 90km/56mi) the route leads through **Rose Valley → p. 64** where the air is heavy with the scent of roses – but, of course, only if you're travelling in May or early June when the bushes are in bloom. From Kazanlak take the E85 into the Balkan Mountains. On the way to Gabrovo there are two outstanding sites: **Shipka Pass → p. 71** and the Etara Open

Photo: A view of the Balkan Mountains

Journeys back in time, tours through hilly terrain and a relaxing Mediterranean atmosphere – get to know the different sides of Bulgaria

Air Museum. The Memorial Church in the small village of **Shipka** and the view from the **Memorial** for fallen Bulgarians and Russians located on the Shipka summit are among the highlights of this route. One option here is to make a 12-km/7-mi detour to the summit of **Buzludzha** east of the Shipka Pass . It's part of a splendid national park and there's also a museum, which resembles a space ship.

The tour comes to a grand finale with a walk through the recreated workshops from the National Revival period in the **Etara Open Air Museum** → p. 70 and can be rounded off with delightful local delicacies available in the wine bar. Virtually immediately behind Etara, up the hill and on the top of a steep rock face you'll find INSIDER TIP Sokolski Monastery, a site as beautiful as it is tranquil. It dates from the middle of the 19th century.

If you'd like to extend the tour by a day, then visit the museum town of **Bozhentsi** → p. 70 and **Trjavna** → p. 71, a village noted for its 19th-century architecture. From there it's not far to **Veliko Tarnovo**

→ p. 66 and **Arbanasi** → p. 70, an impressive village with protected status.

2 RILA AND PIRIN – MOUNTAINS, LAKES AND MONASTERIES

The two highest mountain ranges in the country – Rila and Pirin – are located in the southwest. Both are easily accessible and, with their thick carpet of green and numerous mountain lakes, are amongst the most popular destinations in Bulgaria.

The tour passes through both mountain ranges and provides a good overview of the region's most attractive scenery. At the beginning and end of the tour you'll encounter the world of Bulgarian monasteries. The route, which goes from Rila Monastery via Rila and Bansko to Melnik and to Rozhen Monastery, measures a good 200km/125mi and actual driving time, if you maintain a leisurely pace, is between three and a half and four hours. If you also want to visit Rila Monastery, break the journey in Bansko where there are plenty of good places to spend the night.

The largest, best-known and arguably most beautiful monastery in the country – **Rila Monastery** → p. 41 – is at the beginning of the tour. And allow at least

Melnik, Bulgaria's smallest town

half a day for the visit. The monastery is a symbol of orthodox faith in Bulgaria and the jewel in its crown is the *Sveta Bogorodica* main church.

On the main E79 turn off to the left at Kocherinovo in the direction of Blago-evgrad, and a short detour to **Bansko** → p. 35 is definitely worthwhile. At Sim-itli take a road to the left to Gradevo and Razlog and from the junction it's 43km/28mi. Drive over the Predela Pass that separates the Rila and Pirin Mountains and where locals sell homemade Bulgarian yoghurt, which is definitely worth sampling.

Back on the E79 head south until and just after Sandanski turn off to **Melnik** → p. 42. Allow plenty of time here to take a walk round the smallest town in Bulgaria and also follow the path to the nearby **Rozhen Monastery** → p. 43.

3 ON FOOT: TO THE MOUNTAIN PEAK IN THE BALKANS ☺

Some of the most attractive spots in the Rila and Pirin Mountains can easily be reached on foot, and your efforts will be amply rewarded with a magnificent view from Musala, the highest peak in the Balkans and, with a little bit of luck, you'll also be able to see the Danube and the Aegean.

Allow several days for this mountain hut tour which will take you through the Rila and Pirin Mountains. Make sure you have good hiking equipment, some experience of hill walking is required, plus lots of stamina. Accommodation is very basic up in the mountains, but on the other hand the walk does pass through some pretty areas, otherwise only accessible on foot.

From the south bus station *(Avtogara Yug)* in Sofia take a bus to **Borovets** → p. 40 and from there take the chair lift to the Yastrebets mountain hut, the starting point for the walk. In about two and a half hours you will pass the Musala mountain hut and get to the Everest refuge, situated on a rocky mountain plateau. Just a few metres away is the **Lede-noto Ezero** (Ice Lake), the highest lake (2715m/8908ft) in the Rila Mountains, and even in summer there will be ice floes on the water. The refuge only has sleeping accommodation for 30 people, so it's sensible to make a reservation *(tel. 0888 59 03 42 and 0889 88 18 14)*. From here it only takes half an hour to get to the summit – the important thing to remember is that the earlier you are, the better the view. The walking trail follows a narrow but secure ridge, rocky mountains and deep ravines to the left and right. The ᐳᐸ **Musala** at 2925m/ 9597ft is the highest mountain on the Balkan peninsula and, on good days, or at least so experienced walkers say, you can see as far as the Danube and the Aegean.

This is followed by a five-hour walk to the Granchar mountain hut and then over forest and meadow paths down to the Treshtenik hut. Cross a country road to get to the ● Rhodope railway, a narrow-gauge line which runs three times a day (taking a total of five hours) through the mountain gorges. From the village of Sveta Petka to **Bansko** → p. 35 the journey takes approx. one hour. Stay the night in Bansko, then next day it's six hours to the Demjanitsa (1897m/6224ft) mountain hut. The walking trail runs parallel to the River Demjanitsa and you cross mountain pastures, with the majestic Mount Todorka towering up to the right. Even if the Demjanitsa hut only provides the very basics, spending the night here is a must because it takes some seven hours to get to the Pirin hut. This section forms the second highlight.

The trail goes via the Tevno Ezero refuge *(overnight accommodation, self-catering)* to the Dyasna kraledvorska porta cirque. Pass deep mountain lakes with crystal clear blue water but swimming isn't recommended. The water is rarely warmer than 7°C/45°F and anyway swimming and fishing in the lakes in the Pirin National Park are forbidden. It's worth taking a break at the **Dyasna kraledvorska porta** cirque (approx. 2600m/8530ft) because from here the Vihren and Kutelo Mountains, as well as the impressive Strazhite (The Guards) mountain chain, are visible. Descend from the cirque heading south, the walking trail following the River Zheleznitsa. From here keep heading south until you come to **Rozhen Monastery → p. 43** and then it's not much further to **Melnik → p. 42**. From Melnik take the bus to Sandanski and from there a bus or train back to Sofia.

![number 4 marker]

MEDITERRANEAN AT-MOSPHERE – ALONG THE BLACK SEA COAST

If you want to escape from mass tourism, then high cliffs and white beaches await you on the Black Sea Coast. As you walk along the Black Sea coast from the Romanian to the Turkish border you will encounter unspoilt countryside, a fascinating world of flora and fauna as well as many friendly hosts.

This route covers 378km/235mi along country roads parallel to the coast. The tour begins right up in the north at INSIDER TIP Lake Durankulak, a veritable paradise for nature lovers, amateur archaeologists and bird watchers. Immediately adjacent is the Black Sea. By the ● Kosmos campsite lies one of the widest beaches in the north and is an inviting spot for sunbathing or swimming. The tour then follows the E87 to Shabla where it veers off to the left to the lighthouse and then takes the coast road to ☆ Tjulenovo and **Kamen Bryag → p. 93**. Here the cliffs are high and steep, the turquoise water sparkles, cormorants pose on rocks in the water and sometimes you can even see dolphins at play. Tiny beaches are hidden away in the bays. Just to the south of Kamen Bryag are the next points of interest on this tour: ☆ **Cape Kaliakra → p. 93**, where the E3 walking route ends and **Dalboka mussel farm → p. 93** in a beautiful bay. The latter is also a great place to sample some delicious seafood. In Kavarna return to the main road for a short distance, but you can leave it again at any time to descend to tiny bays and deserted beaches. But detours to the villages of Bozhurets and Topola are also worthwhile. The coast road brings you to **Balchik → p. 92**. This white town by the sea has good tourist facilities, but isn't overrun and it's mainly Bulgarians who spend their summer holidays here.

The tour continues via **Varna** → p. 85, the major city on the Black Sea, in the direction of Burgas. About 25km/15mi south of Varna to the left is the mouth of the Kamchia – a Unesco-listed biosphere reserve, where the river flows through dense primeval forests with a hint of the tropics. All the beaches here are very wide and especially popular with mussel pickers and anglers. Bulgaria's longest beach begins at Camoing Rai and ends at Cape Black *(Cherni nos)*. The village of Shkorpilovtsi offers basic but good accommodation. To the east of the main road lies **Cape Emine**, the easternmost part of the Balkan Mountains, falling almost vertically 60m down into the sea. Around here are hundreds of small rocks which rise up out of the water or lie just beneath it. The nature reserve and the beautiful INSIDER TIP Irakli beach, part of which is designated as a nudist beach, are situated immediately to the north of the cape.

Bulgaria's southern Black Sea coast begins at Cape Emine. Next comes almost at once an architectural gem: the romantic little town of **Nessebar** → p. 83. You really don't need to stop off in the city of Burgas, so arrival at **Sozopol** → p. 85 will come even sooner. To the south of the town the best sandy beaches in Bulgaria stretch out across stunning bays, overlooked by several fine holiday resorts, such as **Kavacite**, **Djuni**, **Arkutino**. The mouth of the **Ropotamo** → p. 83 is a natural curiosity and well worth a visit. The E87 crosses the river south of Sozopol and from now on it gets quieter and quieter. **Tsarevo** has a small and sleepy harbour and **Ahtopol** → p. 83 with its location on a peninsula resembles a miniature version of Sozopol. Some 5km/3mi south of Sinemorets lies INSIDER TIP Silistar beach in a beautiful bay. Here is the last opportunity for a swim before arriving at the Bulgarian-Turkish border at Rezovo.

Sozopol boasts one of the finest beaches on the Black Sea coast

SPORTS & ACTIVITIES

Bulgaria actually has everything or, even better, it has a bit of everything – from high mountains to golden beaches, rivers, lakes, uplands and cultural treasures.

If you want to set off on a tour in Bulgaria, it's best to place yourself in the hands of trained guides. Along the coast many different sports are on offer and there is an infrastructure designed to cater for tourists. If you're interested in extreme sports or an activity holiday, recommended organisers include INSIDER TIP Odysseia-In *(Sofia, Bul. A. Stambolijski 20V | tel. 02 9 89 05 38 | www.odysseia-in.com)* and *Bungee Jumping Varna (Ulitsa Parizhka komuna 18 | tel. 052 60 66 05)* or in Sofia *(Bulevard Sitnjakovo 41 | tel. 02 9 44 44 02 | www.bungy.bg).*

ANGLING

Angling is very popular with many Bulgarians – and not least for the picturesque scenery. From Sofia most people go to the Iskar reservoir and the River Struma; from Burgas to the Kamchia, Tundzha, Ropotamo or Veleka rivers. Many anglers also head for the Black Sea coast. At Golden Sands (port next to the velingrade amphitheatre), you can try your luck off fishing from one of the pleasure boats.

CYCLING

Mountain biking has become very popular in recent years and there's a wide range of organised tours. From the point of view of scenery, the rides through the Rhodopes are

By bike into the mountains, by boat on the Black Sea or by jeep through the wilderness – Bulgaria can supply every kind of sporting activity

the most appealing because the forest is not so dense and the views are better. If you're travelling alone, there's a lovely tour from *Avramovo to Velingrad* (riding time approx. four and a half hours). Organised tours over several days and even one- and two-week tours are also available, for example from the Rhodopes to the Rila and Pirin Mountains *(e.g. Odysseia-In, address p. 100)*.

(e.g. Odysseia-In, address p. 100)

HORSE RIDING

There are numerous attractive bridle paths for horse riders in parts of the Balkans, and especially around Troyan, in the Danube valley and in Rose valley. *Kabiuk Stud,* the biggest stables in Bulgaria, approx. 12km/7mi from Shumen in the village of *Konjovec*, offers an excellent range of facilities and choices. Whether you want to undertake a guided tour or just a short ride on the lunge line, combined with a visit to the adjacent *Stud Museum (Daily 8am–5pm)*, a daytrip to Kabiuk will always prove worthwhile *(tel. 054 5 70 57 | www.kabiuk.*

com). Riding tours are also available in the Rila and Pirin Mountains, e.g. at the *Perivolas Stables* in the village of Bachevo near Razlog and Bansko. This is where the traditional horse races on St Todor's Day are held, the popular festival being celebrated on the Saturday six weeks before Easter *(www.perivolasbg. com | tel. 0888 15 19 66)*.

JEEP SAFARIS

Travel in Russian military jeeps through the Bulgarian interior and enjoy lunch sitting round a camp fire, e.g. in Albena with *Albena Tours (tel. 0579 6 28 48 and tel. 0579 6 28 49)*. Jeep safaris starting from Slanchev Bryag or Zlatni Pyasatsi: *www.safari.kemanbg.com (tel. 0887 98 17 61) or www.columbus-tour.com (tel. 0888 2 70 17)*. Information available in the local hotels.

KAYAK

The country which at times seems so calm and tranquil can also offer the thrills of white water – on the Danube, the Arda, the Struma or through the Iskar Gorge. Tours are organised depending subject to skill level. Rafting tours are also available. *Arzus Canoe-Kayak Club | Stara Zagora | Bulevard Tsar Simeon Veliki 62 | tel. 0886 31 72 51 | www.arzus.dir.bg*

WALKING

Bulgaria has tours to satisfy every taste. If a real sporting challenge is what you are after, then explore the Pirin and Rila Mountains. The trails in the Rila Mountains are soft and green, in the Pirin Mountains on the other hand they're rocky and often very steep. The best time of the year is from July to mid-September, and it's im-

Water-skiing has become a popular activity on the Black Sea

portant to have previous experience of hill walking and be surefooted. Mountain huts on the way provide board and lodging.

If serious hiking is a little too strenuous, then go for a walk to `INSIDER TIP` *Sveta Troitsa* monastery near Veliko Tarnovo (approx. one and a half hours from the north-western side of Trapezica Hill).

Some tours can even be reached by car. Hidden away in the midst of the Rhodopes you'll find the `INSIDER TIP` *Wonderful Bridges* (*Chudnite mostove*), rock formations thousands of years old, rising up at the heart of the secluded forest landscape. *On the road from Smoljan to Plovdiv | approx. 10km/6mi after Chepelare | Turn off towards Zabardo.*

You can enjoy remote countryside on so-called ☺ eco-trails, which will deviate from the well-trodden tourist paths, along rivers, past waterfalls and rock formations. The scenery is for the most part completely unspoilt – no steel, tar or concrete has been used, bridges are made of wood and you climb up and back down on a ladder. The trails are often constructed as a whole-day tour and some are also suitable for families with children. Among the best are the *Rhodopes Eco-trail (Information: Tourist Information Smoljan | tel. 0310 6 25 30)* or the path by the village of Krushuna *(30km/18mi northeast of Lovech on the road to Levski | Turn off right beyond Aleksandrovo)*. The eco-trail is set out as a circular path and leads to a cave and waterfall.

WATERSPORTS

There are countless facilities on the Black Sea coast, with pedalos and rowing boats, water-skiing and windsurfing. The best sailing opportunities are offered by the `INSIDER TIP` *Dinevi Marina* in *Sveti Vlas | Ulitsa Edelvais 39 | Nessebar | tel. 0554 6 40 18 | www.dinevimarina.com*

WELLNESS & SPA TREATMENTS

Valued by the Romans centuries ago, Bulgaria's more than 600 natural mineral springs are still highly regarded today. The therapeutic application of these medicinal springs is available in spa treatment centres, such as in *Velingrad* (131 E3) (*M D7*), *Stara Zagora* (133 D2) (*M H5–6*) and *Sandanski* (130 C5) (*M C8*).

Holidaymakers in search of 'wellness' will get their money's worth in Bulgaria. All the major hotels in the country provide the very latest spa facilities, and relaxing in a mud bath, especially on the Black Sea coast, is popular with the locals. In Pomorie (135 E3) (*M M5*), a resort 20km/12mi northeast of Burgas, many hotels offer `INSIDER TIP` mud treatments. *Interhotel Pomorie | Ulitsa Javorov 3 | tel. 0596 2 24 40 | www.interhotel pomorie.com | Moderate–Expensive*

WINTER SPORTS

The mountains in the south and west of Bulgaria provide good conditions for winter sports fans. Bansko in the Pirin Mountains has become an international ski resort in recent years, and this is where the eastern European free-riding community get together. *Ski and Freeride School OXO | www.oxo.bg | tel. 0887 56 76 72*. In Borovets and Pamporovo there are ski runs for downhill skiing as well as cross-country trails. Winter walks in the Rila and Pirin Mountains are only allowed with a mountain guide. Ask for more information in the ski schools. Away from the ski runs you can ride on a snowmobile, e.g. in Bansko: *www.ban skoskidoo.com | tel. 0878 46 62 62*

TRAVEL WITH KIDS

Bulgarians love children and involve them fully in family life – so they take their little ones with them almost everywhere they go.

Nonetheless, the range of activities for young visitors isn't exactly overwhelming. Yes, it's true there are play areas almost everywhere with sandpits and slides, but that's pretty much all there is. In the large holiday hotels by the Black Sea the situation is better, and here the entertainment programme for children and youngsters of all ages is similar to what you would encounter in western Europe. *www.zade cata.com and deca.start.bg*

KOKOLANDIA ADVENTURE PARK
(0) *(ᗰ C5)*

At the Kokolandia pleasure park in Sofia there's a high-wire course, climbing wall, 9-hole mini-golf course, roundabouts and playgrounds. For children aged 6 and over. *In the Borisova Gradina (behind Hotel Moskva) | 9am–9pm | 3–4 lv per attraction | Ulitsa Nezabravka 15 | www. kokolandia.com*

VARNA DOLPHINARIUM
(129 D5) *(ᗰ N3)*

The dolphinarium in Varna's Sea Garden offers a 40-minute show *(Tue–Sun 10.30am,* midday, 1.30pm and 5pm)* or you can simply watch the marine mammals in their pools or at feeding time. *www.dolphinari um.festa.bg | Admission 16 lv, children 10 lv.*

EATING OUT WITH CHILDREN

Lots of Bulgarian restaurants have their own play areas, so that parents can take their time over a meal. Plovdiv: *Restaurant Evergreen (Ulitsa Vasil Levski and Bulevard Bulgaria).* Sofia: *Restaurant Mocarela Bar (Bulevard Graf Ignatiev 11a).* Varna: *Café 1001 Fairy Tales (Ulitsa Struga, next to Vega, the children's department store).*

INTERACTIVE MUSEUM
(130 C3) *(ᗰ B7)*

Children aged from three to twelve can pretend to be an archaeologist or a scientist, search the ground for buried treasure, restore old pots and observe animals. In the Regional Historical Museum *(Rayonen istoricheski muzei)* in Blagoevgrad there's an interactive exhibition for children. *Ulitsa Rila 1 | Mon–Sat 9am–midday, 1–6pm | Admission 2 lv for 1 adult with 1 child.*

CHILDREN'S ENTERTAINMENT

Children's discos and pony rides, puppet theatres, bungee jumping and tennis,

It could be a pirate adventure, a high-wire course or an interactive museum – if you're travelling with children, there's plenty for everyone to enjoy

mini-golf and computer games, model railways and playgrounds – in the tourist complexes on the Black Sea coast there's so much for children to do, and they're supervised by children's entertainers in Slanchev Bryag, Zlatni Pyasatsi or Albena. Almost every hotel offers a special programme for children and young teenagers.

PALAVNICI CHILDREN'S FAIRGROUND IN SOFIA (0) (🛱 C5)

Adventure playgrounds, roundabouts, miniature railway, puppet theatre, a café with children's menus – Palavnici provides fun for all the family, in summer and winter. *Wed–Sun | Sofia Mladost 3 | Bulevard Filip Avramov | Day ticket 20 lv | www.palavnici-bg.com*

PIRATE ADVENTURE (129 E5) (🛱 N3)

Oh to be a pirate! To sail the seven seas, search for buried treasure and fight mutineers! All of that and more is possible on the *Leonardo (Travelpartner | Hotel Magnolia in Golden Sands | tel. 052*

38 25 50 | 50 lv). Half-day trips on a pirate ship are available from Albena. The children are supervised by entertainers and dress up as pirates, hoist the skull and cross bones and set off in search of treasure. Adults, in the meantime, can go fishing. Food and drink on board. You can get more information from the hotels in Albena *(www.albena.bg | 30 lv per child, 60 lv per adult)*.

PUPPET THEATRE

There are puppet theatres in many towns. Sofia: *Ulitsa Gen. Josif V. Gurko 14 (U C–D4) (🛱 c–d4)* and *Bulevard Janko Sakasov 19 (U F3) (🛱 f3) | tel. 02 9 88 54 16 | www.sofiapuppet.com.* Varna: *Ulitsa Dragoman 4 | tel. 052 60 78 44 | www.vnpuppet.com.* Plovdiv: *Ulitsa Hristo G. Danov 14 | tel. 032 62 32 75 | www.pptheatre.com.* Ruse: *Ulitsa Knjazheska 9 | tel. 082 22 52 73 | puppetruse.com.* Performances mainly at weekends, but also during the week. *(4–8 lv)*

FESTIVALS & EVENTS

In Bulgaria the main holidays are at Easter and Christmas but the National Liberation Day on 3 March and the National Day of Culture (24 May) are also considered important dates. Bulgarians celebrate their saints days exuberantly and most Muslims also observe the Islamic religious holidays.

OFFICIAL HOLIDAYS

1 Jan New Year; **3 March** National Liberation Day; **Easter Monday** (date determined by the Orthodox calendar); **1 May** May Day; **6 May** Bulgarian Army Day; **24 May** National Day of Culture, also popularly known as the Cyrillic Alphabet Day; **6 Sept** Unification Day; **22 Sept** Independence Day; **1 Nov** National Revival Day; **24, 25/26 Dec** Christmas

FESTIVALS & EVENTS

There are numerous jazz, folk and classical music festivals. The Bulgarians particularly like the so-called ▶ INSIDERTIP *Sabori*, traditional festivals as celebrated in the rural areas with lots of music, dancing, eating and drinking.

FEBRUARY

On the Saturday six weeks before Easter ▶ *St Todor's Day (Todorovden)* is celebrated throughout Bulgaria. Traditional festivals take place in the village squares in honour of St Todor, the patron saint of horses and horsemen, and horse races are also held.

MARCH/APRIL

1. March: ▶ *Start of spring*. People present one another with a ▶ *Martenica*, two small, red and white tassels on the ends of a red and white braided thread. It's worn on clothing or round the wrist or neck and should not be taken off until the recipient has seen a stork.

March: ▶ *Start of Lent.* Men in animal costumes *(kukeri)* and adorned with fertility symbols pass through the village and dance in the village square.

Middle of March: ▶ *Sofia International Film Festival*. Nine cinemas in Sofia show films, documentaries, cartoons and shorts, ranging from blockbusters to low budget films to experimental cinema. Competitions are held and the best films nominated. In Bulgaria foreign films are usually shown in the original language with subtitles.

March: International Festival ▶ *Martenski musikalni Dni* for orchestral and chamber music and opera in Ruse

Eight days before Easter Sunday: ▶ *La-*

Not just classical music, jazz and opera – Bulgarians also love to showcase their roses and their celebrated yoghurt

zarovden is an expression of the longing for fertility and a chance to look for a bride, with young girls in national costume singing and dancing.

MAY

6 May: ▶ *Georgievden:* Bulgarian Army Day, with military parades and festivities everywhere.

In odd years: ▶ *Festival of Humour and Satire* in Gabrovo

▶ INSIDER TIP ▶ 21 May: *Nestinarstvo:* on the name day of St Constantine and St Elena, dancers perform barefoot on glowing coals; mainly in the southeast (Balgari, Brodilovo, Rezovo)

MAY–JULY

▶ *Sofiiski musikalni Sedmizi:* Festival of classical and modern orchestral music in Sofia

JUNE

Start of the month: ▶ *Rose Festival* in Karlovo and Kazanlak. Rose harvest traditions.

Mid-June to mid-August ▶ ★ *Varna Summer:* classical music, opera and ballet – a renowned festival with distinguished ensembles from all over the world; a ballet competition every two years

JULY

▶ *Yoghurt Festival* in Razgrad. Thanks to 'Lactobazillus bulgaricus', Bulgarian natural yoghurt is known well beyond the country's borders. Made from fermented milk, it is also served in pubs and restaurants.

AUGUST

▶ *Folklore Festival* in Koprivshtitsa, a mix of pop festival and medieval funfair

▶ ● INSIDER TIP ▶ *International Jazz Festival in Banska*, always from 8 to 13 August

SEPTEMBER

▶ *Apollonia Festival of Arts* in Sozopol on the Black Sea coast

LINKS, BLOGS, APPS & MORE

LINKS

▶ http://bulgariatravel.org The Official Tourism Portal of Bulgaria provides comprehensive information about all aspects of the country from the tourist's point of view. Many fine pictures included. It's available in English and eight other languages

▶ www.online.bg Website with the latest information on politics and the economy and links to the Yellow Pages and telephone directory. In Bulgarian and English

▶ paper.standartnews.com/en This national newspaper based in Sofia publishes an internet edition in Bulgarian and English

▶ www.programata.bg Countless tips about theatre productions, concerts, exhibitions and cinema programmes for Sofia, Plovdiv, Varna, Burgas and Stara Zagora. It also contains a list of restaurants, bars and clubs. All in English

▶ www.peakview.bg An attractive site which is user-friendly and not overloaded with information. Many interesting links with a focus on outdoor activities

BLOGS & FORUMS

▶ www.travellerspoint.com/blogs Enter Bulgaria in the search field and read the personal experiences of experienced travellers. Photos and useful links

▶ http://abritinbulgaria.blogspot.co.uk This site is written by an English businessman who's lived and worked in Bulgaria for six years

▶ www.travelblog.org/Europe/Bulgaria Thousands of photos and comments, plus travel and tourist information

▶ sofiadailyphoto.blogspot.com A Bulgarian woman called Antonia who lives in Sofia posts a new picture every day – her evocative images convey the atmosphere of Bulgaria's capital

Regardless of whether you are still preparing your trip or already in Bulgaria: these addresses will provide you with more information, videos and networks to make your holiday even more enjoyable.

▶ www.motoroads.com/bulgaria-travel-video.aspx If you're travelling round Bulgaria by car or motorbike, then do have a look at this site. Videos show touring bikers and jeeps out in the wild and there's also a film (video no. 6) on the '24 Wonders of Bulgaria', Thracian tombs (video no. 4) and much more

▶ YouTube 'Kalofer' and 'horo' are the words you need to find this video, which shows men dancing the traditional horo in the ice cold waters of the River Tundzha on 6 January to celebrate Epiphany

▶ YouTube Enter 'Bulgaria vs Europe' in the YouTube search field. The Bulgarians love to laugh, mostly about themselves. This amusing animated video compares Bulgaria with Europe, with regard to parking, work, relations with neighbours...

▶ SkiBulgaria An app providing information about the Bulgarian ski resorts with up-to-date maps, weather, snow conditions and ski lift operations. It also shows pictures from live cameras. With GPS support

▶ BG Radio Bulgaria The music will lift your spirits. Download the best Bulgarian pop and rock songs directly from BG Radio's app

▶ Bulgaria Travel Guide Everything you need to know about towns and cities, transport, shopping, food and drink, hotels and lots more. With this app you can also get detailed information about Burgas, Plovdiv, Ruse, Sofia and Varna on your smart phone

▶ www.facebook.com/bulgariatravelorg The English language Facebook site of Bulgaria's Official Tourism Portal provides picture galleries, proposed tours and videos, and members exchange their news and opinions.

▶ www.tripadvisor.co.uk This popular site does not need any introduction. Search under Reviews for insider information on hotels, B&Bs and restaurants. The Forum pages are also very informative. Plus countless good pictures.

TRAVEL TIPS

ARRIVAL

🚗 The shortest route by car from London to Bulgaria is via Brussels, Frankfurt, Munich, Vienna, Budapest, Belgrade and Niš or alternatively via Graz in Austria, and then Maribor, Zagreb, Belgrade and Niš, then on to Sofia. You can also drive through Romania via Timișoara and Calafat and then by ferry across the Danube to Vidin. This route is longer and there are fewer motorways. Another way to get there, but more time-consuming, is to travel via Italy (Trieste, Venice, Ancona) and then by ferry to Greece and via Thessaloniki to Sofia.

🚆 The shortest rail links to Sofia are via Vienna and Belgrade (changing twice) or via Budapest (once). From London the journey to Sofia via Vienna/Belgrade takes approx. 38 hours, via Budapest approx. 42 hours.

🚌 Some bus companies offer scheduled services to Sofia.

✈ Currently there are direct scheduled flights to Sofia with easyJet, British Airways, WizzAir and Bulgaria Air and some of these airlines also fly to Plovdiv, Varna and Burgas. There are charter flights in the summer serving the airports in Varna and Burgas and in the winter to the airports situated near the mountains in the interior. There are no direct flights to Bulgaria from the USA.

BANKS & MONEY

Unlimited amounts of domestic and foreign currency may be brought into the country. If you want to change money, you should do so in a bank, not on the black market. ATMs are widespread, and you'll get the best exchange rate if you withdraw money from cash machines with a credit card. All major credit cards are accepted in the larger hotels, car hire offices and some shops and restaurants.

CAMPING

The country has an extensive network of campsites, but be aware that, since government funding was withdrawn, facilities can be rather run-down. You'll find at least one in the places which attract tourists and, on the Black Sea, there are plenty to choose from all along the coast, although they tend to be very crowded in July and August.

CAR HIRE

There are plenty of car rental offices, mainly in the tourist centres. Daily charg-

RESPONSIBLE TRAVEL

It doesn't take a lot to be environmentally friendly whilst travelling. Don't just think about your carbon footprint whilst flying to and from your holiday destination but also about how you can protect nature and culture abroad. As a tourist it is especially important to respect nature, look out for local products, cycle instead of driving, save water and much more. If you would like to find out more about eco-tourism please visit: *www.ecotourism.org*

es for small to medium-sized cars start from approx. 60 leva plus mileage. Credit cards are generally accepted. Car hire offers can be found for example at *www. rentacarbulgaria.com*.

CLIMATE, WHEN TO GO

Bulgaria enjoys a continental climate with hot summers and cold, often damp winters. Southern Bulgaria and the region around Ruse have the highest temperatures. Rainfall is highest in the mountains.

On the Black Sea Coast the winters are mild. The best time to travel is between April and mid-June and in September when the land is green and temperatures pleasant and off-peak prices apply. The summer (the middle of June till the start of September) is ideal for a beach holiday, walking and festivals, though temperatures can be very high and only in the mountains is it cooler. The peak season on the Black Sea coast is between the middle of July and the end of August. September is one of the best months to visit Bulgaria. Fruit and vegetables are readily available and mass tourism is past its peak. There's a summer warmth, but it's nowhere near as hot. As soon as the first snow falls (around the middle of December), many Bulgarians and tourists head for the ski resorts, some of which stay open until mid-April. The peak season for winter sports is around Christmas and the New Year, and also between the start of February and the middle of March.

CONSULATES & EMBASSIES

UK EMBASSY IN SOFIA
9 Moskovska Street | Sofia 1000 | tel. 02 9 33 92 22 | http://ukinbulgaria.fco.gov. uk/en/

US EMBASSY IN SOFIA
16, Kozyak Street | Sofia 1408 | tel. 02 9 37 51 00 | http://bulgaria.usembassy.gov

CUSTOMS

The import and export of cash above 20,000 leva as well as valuables (e.g. jewellery or video cameras) must be declared in writing to Bulgarian customs, where the relevant forms are available. The copy of the declaration must be kept until you leave the country. If you're travelling privately, you may bring in items for your own use without limit, but please note the following restrictions per adult apply: max. 200 cigarettes; spirits up to 1l (over 22%) or 2l (below 22%).

BUDGETING

Coffee	0.25–1.60 £ / 0.40–2.50 $	*for a cup of espresso*
Snack	0.30–0.50 £ / 0.40–0.75 $	*for a banica*
Wine	0.80–2.50 £ / 1.30–3.80 $	*for a glass of wine*
Parasol	1.60–6.40 £ / 2.50–10.00 $	*hire charge per day*
Petrol	0.80–1.00 £ / 1.20–1.60 $	*for 1l super lead-free*
Taxi	0.20–1.60 £ / 0.40–2.50 $	*per kilometre*

DRIVING

Always carry your national driving licence and do remember to obtain an international green insurance card in advance. It is obligatory. Otherwise you'll have to buy third party insurance at the border. A police report is necessary should you need to make an insurance claim. Maximum speeds: car on motorways 130km/h, on main roads 90km/h, in built-up areas 50km/h; car with caravan and motorbikes 100/70/50km/h.

Using a phone in a car is only allowed with a hands-free device. You must drive on dipped headlights during the day from 1 November till 1 March. Blood alcohol content maximum: 0.5 mg per 100 ml. For motorway travel, cars, motorbikes and camper vans need a windscreen sticker, which can be bought at all the border crossings in three different forms: seven days cost 10 leva, a month 26 leva and a year 68 leva.

The breakdown service requires the emergency phone number 02 9 11 46 or 146. The *Sajus na Balgarskite Avtomobilisti SBA in Sofia (Ploshtad Pozitano 3 | tel. 02 9 35 79 35 | www.uab.org)* manages the central breakdown service. Be aware that car theft is quite common and foreign cars are a popular target. Always allow plenty of time for your journey as road conditions can be difficult, with many potholes, roads still under construction or repair and farm traffic. And make sure you have a good map because many road signs are only in the Cyrillic script.

CURRENCY CONVERTER

£	LEVA	LEVA	£
1	2.42	1	0.41
2	4.84	2	0.82
5	12	5	2.06
7	17	10	4.12
15	36.35	20	8.24
25	60	30	12.40
30	73	50	20.60
50	121	100	41
100	242	500	206

$	LEVA	LEVA	$
1	1.50	1	0.66
2	3	2	1.32
5	7.55	5	3.30
7	10.57	10	6.62
15	22.65	20	13.24
25	38	30	20
30	45	50	33
50	75	100	66
100	151	500	331

For current exchange rates see www.xe.com

EMERGENCY SERVICES

Emergency services *tel. 112,* fire brigade *tel. 160,* emergency doctor *tel. 150,* police *tel. 166*

HEALTH

Medical care in the major hospitals is good, although there's a lack of modern medical equipment. Doctors at bolnitsa (state hospitals) usually speak English. Emergency treatment can normally be directly settled by insurance, but EU residents must present the European Health Insurance card (EHIC – obtainable online or phone 0845 606 2030). Many of the medicines common in the UK and US can be obtained in Bulgarian pharmacies.

IMMIGRATION

EU citizens and US Americans can enter the country with a valid passport and a visa is not required. Children under 16 must also hold a passport. If you're staying longer than 90 days, you must register with the Bulgarian police and apply for a residence permit.

INFORMATION

BULGARIAN UK EMBASSY
186-188 Queen's Gate | London SW7 5HL | tel. 0207 5 84 94 00 | http://www.bulgar ianembassy-london.org

BULGARIAN UK EMBASSY COMMERCIAL SECTION
186-188 Queen's Gate | London SW7 5HL | tel. 0207 5 89 84 02 | www.bulgariatravel.org

BULGARIAN US EMBASSY
1621 22nd Street | NW, Washington D.C. 20008 | tel. 020 4 83 13 86 | office@bul garia-embassy.org

INTERNET

The most informative internet portals for everything to do with Bulgaria are *www. dir.bg, www.online.bg* and *www.search. bg*, both in Bulgarian and English. You'll also find plenty of information about all tourist matters at *www.discover-bulgaria. com* and *www.bulgariatravel.org*. There is a good selection of hotels at *www.ho telbg.com* and *www.hotelite.net*, and in most cases you can make online bookings. For restaurants and bars try *www. restaurant.bg* and *shaker.dir.bg*, discos and nightclubs *www.disco.bg*. A relatively good overview of tourism on the Black Sea coast can be obtained at *www. beachbulgaria.com*. The news websites *www.novinite.com* and *www.sofiaecho. com* provide news about current politics, and also general information. Some towns and cities already have their own internet presence. You can find events

A field of sunflowers near Kotel

information and cultural tips at *www. programata.bg* and *www.cult.bg*. Almost all the major hotels provide wi-fi.

INTERNET CAFÉS

In all the larger towns and cities there's at least one small internet café, though it has to be said the computer equipment and software are often rudimentary. Many of the hotels at Golden Sands and Sunny Beach have their own internet cafés. Sofia: *Internet Centre Garibaldi | Ulitsa Graf Ignatiev 6 (U C4) (*∭ *c4)* – Varna: *BGZone | Ulitsa Kjustendzha 24* – Plovdiv: *Internet Club Neo | Ulitsa Raiko Daskalov 48; Internet Club Fantasy | Ulitsa Knjaz Aleksandar Batemberg, 31*

LANGUAGE

Bulgarian is a southern Slav language which is written in Cyrillic script. In this book the Bulgarian names and words have been transposed into Latin script and standard spellings guided by English have been used so that you can find the names on the internet. The standard Bulgarian system for converting to Latin script, e.g. on place names and street signs, was also followed.

OPENING HOURS

As a rule food stores are open Monday to Friday from 8am till 8pm, clothes shops from 10am till 7pm and banks from 9am till 4pm. Supermarkets, shopping centres and small shops are also open on Saturday. In almost all the larger towns and cities, you'll find food stores that are open round the clock Monday to Sunday. Post offices are usually open Monday to Saturday from 8am till 6pm. You can buy stamps there and also at some kiosks.

PHONE & MOBILE PHONE

Hotels often provide local calls at very reasonable prices and in Sofia some calls are free. However, international calls can be expensive. Dialling codes: *0044* to the UK, *001* to US, *00359* from Europe to Bulgaria, followed by the relevant city code without the zero.

When using a mobile phone, you save money on roaming if you choose the cheapest network. There are no charges for incoming calls with a Bulgarian prepaid card, which you can buy in your resort. The most frequently used providers are M-Tel and Globul and you can buy their SIM cards in their own shops in all the large towns and cities, but also in many of the smaller towns and villages.

You can buy prepaid cards before you leave and, although they're expensive, they too can offer considerable savings on roaming.

PHOTOGRAPHY

Most Bulgarians are happy to be photographed and accept it in laissez-faire style. Taking photos of military installations and border crossings is prohibited. The custom in churches can vary, so check in advance. Digital memory cards are widely available.

PRICES & CURRENCY

The unit of currency is the lev (usually abbreviated to lv in this book; plural leva; 1 lev = 100 stotinki) and it's closely tied to the euro. Exchange rates in the tourist centres are usually less favourable. Generally speaking, prices for tourists are low, as long as you avoid the hotels in the major cities, holiday centres and international car rental companies. Private accommodation can be had for as little as 20 leva per night, but bear in mind that accommodation prices are subject to season and demand. In some museums, different admission charges apply for local and foreign visitors. There's no admission charge for the monasteries, though small donations are always welcome.

PUBLIC TRANSPORT

There's an extensive network both for inner-city transport as well as long distance travel, and prices are very reasonable. For longer journeys the bus is usually preferable to the train; you can enquire about the bus operators in the large hotels. It is generally advisable to stick with the main companies: Etap Adress/Grup *(etapgroup.com)* and Biomet *(www.biomet-bg.com)*. Departure times are displayed at the central bus stations. There are domestic flights between Sofia and Varna, and between Sofia and Burgas.

TAXI

A taxi meter is compulsory, as is a receipt. A notice with the cost per kilometre must be clearly displayed on the front windscreen or on the side window. Agree the full fare with the taxi driver before you accept a ride.

TIME

Bulgaria uses Eastern European time (EET), in other words it is two hours ahead of GMT. Moving the clock forward to summer time in March and back in October coincides with the changes in central Europe and the UK.

WI-FI

Most public buildings in the major cities and on the Black Sea coast have wi-fi internet access, as do many hotels, some restaurants, cafés, markets and the OMV filling stations around Sofia.

WEATHER IN VARNA

	Jan	Feb	March	April	May	June	July	Aug	Sept	Oct	Nov	Dec
Daytime temperatures in °C/°F	4/40	6/43	10/50	15/59	21/70	26/79	29/84	29/84	24/75	20/68	13/55	7/45
Nighttime temperatures in °C/°F	−2/28	−2/28	2/36	7/45	12/54	16/61	18/64	17/63	14/57	10/50	6/43	0/32
Sunshine hours/day	3	3	4	6	8	10	11	11	8	5	3	3
Precipitation days/month	6	5	5	5	7	8	6	3	4	5	6	7
Water temperature in °C/°F	6/43	6/43	7/45	10/50	15/59	19/66	22/72	23/73	21/70	17/63	13/55	9/48

NOTES

MARCO POLO TRAVEL GUIDES

ALGARVE
AMSTERDAM
ATHENS
AUSTRALIA
BANGKOK
BARCELONA
BERLIN
BRAZIL
BRUSSELS
BUDAPEST
BULGARIA
CALIFORNIA
CAMBODIA
CAPE TOWN
  WINE LANDS,
  GARDEN ROUTE
CHINA
COLOGNE
COPENHAGEN
CORFU
COSTA BLANCA
  VALENCIA
COSTA DEL SOL
  GRANADA
CRETE
CUBA
CYPRUS
  NORTH AND
  SOUTH
DUBAI

DUBLIN
DUBROVNIK &
  DALMATIAN COAST
EDINBURGH
EGYPT
FINLAND
FLORENCE
FLORIDA
FRENCH ATLANTIC
  COAST
FRENCH RIVIERA
  NICE, CANNES &
  MONACO
FUERTEVENTURA
GRAN CANARIA
GREECE
HONG KONG
  MACAU
ICELAND
IRELAND
ISRAEL
ISTANBUL
JORDAN
KOS
KRAKOW
LAKE GARDA

LANZAROTE
LAS VEGAS
LISBON
LONDON
LOS ANGELES
MADEIRA
  PORTO SANTO
MADRID
MALLORCA
MALTA
  GOZO
MAURITIUS
MILAN
MOROCCO
MUNICH
NAPLES &
  THE AMALFI COAST
NEW YORK
NEW ZEALAND
NORWAY
OSLO
PARIS
PORTUGAL

PRAGUE
RHODES
ROME
SAN FRANCISCO
SARDINIA
SCOTLAND
SHANGHAI
SICILY
SINGAPORE
SOUTH AFRICA
STOCKHOLM
TENERIFE
THAILAND
TURKEY
TURKEY
  SOUTH COAST
TUSCANY
UNITED ARAB
  EMIRATES
VENICE
VIENNA
VIETNAM

MARCO POLO

MARCO POLO

ROAD ATLAS & PULL-OUT MAP

KE GARDA

With STREET ATLAS & PULL-OUT MAP

EW YORK

MARCO POLO

With ROAD ATLAS & PULL-OUT MAP

FRENCH RIVIERA
NICE, CANNES & MONACO

SPECTACULAR GRAND CANYON DU VERDON
Breath-taking scenery that takes some beating

SNIFFING THE AIR
The perfume manufacturers of Grasse

Insider
Tips

www.marco-polo.com

MARCO POLO

With ROAD ATLAS & PULL-OUT MAP

ALLORCA

With STREET ATLAS & PULL-OUT MAP

BERLIN

A STUNNING ISLAND JUST FOR ART
wcasing treasures from around the world

OOL AT NIGHT
tin club scene sets the trend

Insider
Tips

* PACKED WITH INSIDER TIPS
* BEST WALKS AND TOURS
* FULL-COLOUR PULL-OUT MAP
  AND STREET ATLAS

USEFUL PHRASES BULGARIAN

PRONUNCIATION

Bulgarian is written in Cyrillic. To aid pronunciation all words are accompanied by a simple transliteration (in the middle column).
It is important that words with more than one syllable have the correct intonation. The stressed syllable is signified by an accent.
Further note that zh is pronounced like the 's' in pleasure or conclusion and that ŭ is like the 'u' in sun.

IN BRIEF

Yes/No/Maybe	da/ne/mozhé bi	Да/Не/Може би
Please/Thank you	mólya/blagodaryá	Моля./Благодаря
Excuse me, please	izwinéte	Извинете
May I ...?	móga li ...?	Мога ли?
Pardon?	mólya?	Моля?
I would like to .../	ískam da .../	Искам да .../
have you got ...?	ímate li ...?	Имате ли ...?
How much is ...?	kólko strúva ...?	Колко струва ...?
I (don't) like this)	tová (ne) mi kharésva	Това (не) ми харесва
good/bad	dobró/lósho	добро/лошо
too much/much/little	mnógo e/mnógo/málko	много е/много/малко
all/nothing	vsíchko/níshto	всичко/нищо
Help!/Attention!	pómosht!/vnimánie!	Помощ!/Внимание!
ambulance	lineĭka	линейка
police/fire brigade	polítsya/pozharna	полиция/пожарна
Prohibition/forbidden	zabrána/zabranéno e	забрана/забранено е
Danger/dangerous	opásnost/opásno e	опасност/опасно е

GREETINGS, FAREWELL

Good morning!/	dobró útro!/	Добро утро!/
Good afternoon!/	dobŭr den!/	Добър ден!/
Good evening!/	dobŭr vécher!/	Добър вечер!/
Good night!	léka nosht!	Лека нощ!
Hello!/Goodbye!	sdraveĭ/dovízhdane!	Здравей!/Довиждане!
My name is ...	az se kázvam	Аз се казвам...
What's your name?	vie kak se kázvate?/	Вие как се казвате?/
	ti kak se kázvash?	Ти как се казваш?

Говорите ли български?

'Do you speak Bulgarian?' This guide will help you to say the basic words and phrases in Bulgarian.

DATE & TIME

Monday/Tuesday	ponedélnik/wtórnik	понеделник/вторник
Wednesday/Thursday	sryáda/chetvŭrtak	сряда/четвъртък
Friday/Saturday	petŭk/sŭbota	петък/събота
Sunday/working day	nedélya/rabóten den	неделя/работен ден
today/tomorrow/yesterday	dnes/útre/vchéra	днес/утре/вчера
What time is it?	kólko e chasŭt	Колко е часът?
It's three o'clock	chasŭt e tri	Часът е три
It's half past three	chasŭt e tri i polovína	Часът е три и половина
a quarter to four	chétiri bez petnádeset	Четири без петнадесет
a quarter past four	chétiri i petnádeset	Четири и петнадесет

TRAVEL

open/closed	otvóreno/zatvóreno	отворено/затворено
entrance/exit	vkhod/ízkhod	вход/изход
toilets/restrooms/	toalétni/	тоалетни/
ladies/gentlemen	zhení/mŭzhé	жени/мъже
(no) drinking water	(ne e) vóda za píene	(не е) вода за пиене
Where is ...?/	kŭdé e ...?/	Къде е ...?/
Where are ...?	kadé sa ...?	Къде са ...?
left/right	lyávo/dyásno	ляво/дясно
straight ahead/back	naprávo/nazád	направо/назад
bus/tram/	avtobús/tramvaĭ/	автобус/трамвай/
underground / taxi/cab	metró/taksí	метро/такси
train station/harbour	gára/pristánishte	гара/пристанище
airport	letíshte	летище
schedule/ticket	razpisánie/bilét	разписание/билет
train/platform	vlak/kolovóz	влак/коловоз
I would like to rent ...	zheláya da vzéma po náem	Желая да взема по наем ...
a car/a bicycle	avtomobíl/velosipéd	автомобил/велосипед
a boat	lódka	лодка
petrol/gas station	benzinostántsiya	бензиностанция

FOOD & DRINK

Could you please book a table for tonight for four?	mólya da ní rezervírate za tázi vécher edná mása za chetiríma	Моля да ни резервирате за тази вечер една маса за четирима

The menu, please	menyúto mólya	Менюто, моля
Could I please have ...?	móga li da porŭtcham ...?	Мога ли да поръчам ...?
May I have the bill, please?	áko obícháte smétkata	Ако обичате, сметката

SHOPPING

I'd like .../I'm looking for ...	az ískam .../az tŭrsya...	Аз искам .../Аз търся ...
pharmacy/chemist	aptéka/drogériya	аптека/дрогерия
shopping centre/	mol/	мол/
department store	universálen magazín	универсален магазин
supermarket	súpermárket	супермаркет
kiosk	pavilión	павилион
expensive/cheap/price	skŭpo/évtino/tsená	скъпо/евтино/цена
more/less	póveche/po-málko	повече/по-малко

ACCOMMODATION

Do you have any ... left?	ímate li óshte ...	Имате ли още ...
single room	ediníchni stái	единични стаи
double room	dwóini stái	двойни стаи
breakfast/half board	zakúska/polúpansión	закуска/полупансион
full board	pŭlen pansión/	пълен пансион/
(American plan)	ol ínkluziv	ол инклузив
shower/sit-down bath	dush/bánya	душ/баня

BANKS, MONEY & CREDIT CARDS

bank/ATM/Geldautomat	bánka/bankomát	банка/банкомат
pin code	pin kod	пин код
I'd like to change ...	az ískam ... da smenyá	Аз искам ... да сменя
cash/	v broí/	в брой/
credit card	kréditna karta	кредитна карта
bill/coin	banknóta/monéta	банкнота/монета

HEALTH

doctor/dentist/	lékar/zubolékar/	лекар/зъболекар/
paediatrician	détski lékar	детски лекар
hospital/	bólnitsa/	болница/бърза
emergency clinic	bŭrsa pómosht	помощ
fever/pain	temperatúra/bólki	температура/болки
diarrhoea/	rastroístvo/	разстройство/
nausea	lósho mi e	лошо ми е
sunburn	slŭnchevo izgáryane	слънчево изгаряне
inflamed/injured	vŭzpaléno/naranéno	възпалено/наранено
plaster/bandage	lekoplást/prevrŭzka	лекопласт/превръзка

pain reliever/ tablet/suppository	obezbolyávashto/ tabletka/sveshtichka	обезболяващо/ таблетка/свещичка

POST, TELECOMMUNICATIONS & MEDIA

stamp/ letter	póshtenska márka/ pismó	пощенска марка/ писмо
postcard	póshtenska kártichka	пощенска картичка
I'm looking for a prepaid card for my mobile	Tŭrsya predplaténa kárta za móya mobílen telefón	Търся предплатена карта за моя мобилен телефон
socket/adapter	kontátkt/adápter	контакт/адаптер
computer/battery/ rechargeable battery	kompyutŭr/batéri ya/ akumulátor	компютър/батерия/ акумулатор
e-mail address	adrés za elektrónna póshta	адрес за електронна поща
internet connection/ wi-fi	internet dóstŭp/ bezzhíchen internet	интернет достъп/ безжичен интернет
e-mail/file/ print	imeïl/faïl/ razpechátvam	имейл/файл/ разпечатвам

LEISURE, SPORTS & BEACH

beach/lido	bryág/plazh	бряг/плаж
sunshade/ lounger	plázhen chadŭr/ zhezlóng	плажен чадър/ жезлонг
cable car/chair lift	vŭzhena líniya/lift	въжена линия/лифт
(rescue) hut	(podslón) khízha	(подслон) хижа

NUMBERS

0	núla	нула	15	petnájset	петнадесет
1	ednó	едно	16	schestnájset	шестнадесет
2	dve	две	17	sedemnájset	седемнадесет
3	tri	три	18	osemnájset	осемнадесет
4	chetiri	четири	19	dewetnájset	деветнадесет
5	pet	пет	70	sedemdesét	седемдесет
6	shest	шест	80	osemdesét	осемдесет
7	sédem	седем	90	dewedesét	деведесет
8	ósem	осем	100	sto	сто
9	dévet	девет	200	dwésta	двеста
10	déset	десет	1000	chiljáda	хиляда
11	edinádeset	единадесет	2000	dwé chiljadi	две хиляди
12	dvanádeset	дванадесет	10000	déset chiljadi	десет хиляди
13	trinádeset	тринадесет	½	edná polowína	една половина
14	chetirinádeset	четиринадесет	¼	edná tschétwart	една четвърт

ROAD ATLAS

The green line   indicates the Trips & Tours (p. 94–99)
The blue line   indicates The perfect route (p. 30–31)

All tours are also marked on the pull-out map

Photo: Tetrasiada fortress, Kaliakra

Exploring Bulgaria

The map on the back cover shows how the area has been sub-divided

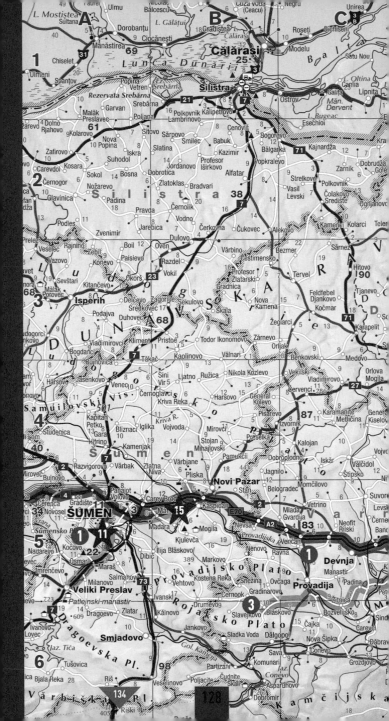

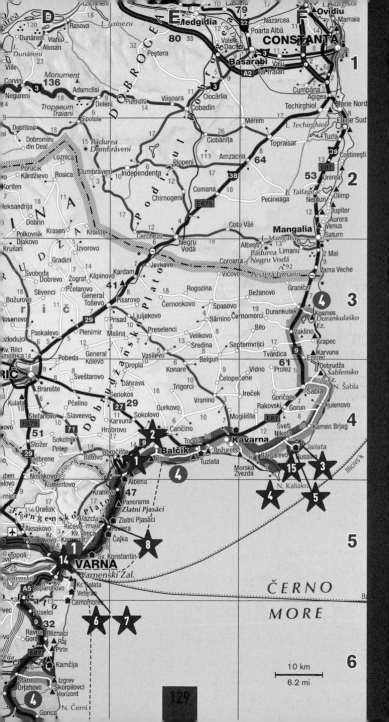

KEY TO ROAD ATLAS

18 26	Autobahn mit Anschlussstellen	Motorway with junctions
	Autobahn in Bau	Motorway under construction
I	Mautstelle	Toll station
O	Raststätte mit Übernachtung	Roadside restaurant and hotel
	Raststätte	Roadside restaurant
	Tankstelle	Filling-station
	Autobahnähnliche Schnell-straße mit Anschlussstelle	Dual carriage-way with motorway characteristics with junction
	Fernverkehrsstraße	Trunk road
	Durchgangsstraße	Thoroughfare
	Wichtige Hauptstraße	Important main road
	Hauptstraße	Main road
	Nebenstraße	Secondary road
	Eisenbahn	Railway
	Autozug-Terminal	Car-loading terminal
	Zahnradbahn	Mountain railway
	Kabinenschwebebahn	Aerial cableway
	Eisenbahnfähre	Railway ferry
	Autofähre	Car ferry
	Schifffahrtslinie	Shipping route
	Landschaftlich besonders schöne Strecke	Route with beautiful scenery
Alleenstr.	Touristenstraße	Tourist route
XI-V	Wintersperre	Closure in winter
	Straße für Kfz gesperrt	Road closed to motor traffic
8%	Bedeutende Steigungen	Important gradients
	Für Wohnwagen nicht empfehlenswert	Not recommended for caravans
	Für Wohnwagen gesperrt	Closed for caravans
☀	Besonders schöner Ausblick	Important panoramic view

* *Wartenstein* * *Umbalfälle*	Sehenswert: Kultur - Natur	Of interest: culture - nature
	Badestrand	Bathing beach
	Nationalpark, Naturpark	National park, nature park
	Sperrgebiet	Prohibited area
	Kirche	Church
	Kloster	Monastery
	Schloss, Burg	Palace, castle
	Moschee	Mosque
	Ruinen	Ruins
	Leuchtturm	Lighthouse
	Turm	Tower
∩	Höhle	Cave
	Ausgrabungsstätte	Archaeological excavation
▲	Jugendherberge	Youth hostel
▲	Allein stehendes Hotel	Isolated hotel
⌂	Berghütte	Refuge
▲	Campingplatz	Camping site
	Flughafen	Airport
	Regionalflughafen	Regional airport
⊕	Flugplatz	Airfield
	Staatsgrenze	National boundary
	Verwaltungsgrenze	Administrative boundary
⊖	Grenzkontrollstelle	Check-point
⊖	Grenzkontrollstelle mit Beschränkung	Check-point with restrictions
ROMA	Hauptstadt	Capital
VENÉZIA	Verwaltungssitz	Seat of the administration
	Ausflüge & Touren	Trips & Tours
	Perfekte Route	Perfect route
★ 1	MARCO POLO Highlight	MARCO POLO Highlight

INDEX

The index lists all the sights and destinations featured in this guide. Page numbers in bold indicate a main entry.

WRITE TO US

e-mail: info@marcopologuides.co.uk

Did you have a great holiday?
Is there something on your mind?
Whatever it is, let us know!
Whether you want to praise, alert us to errors or give us a personal tip –
MARCO POLO would be pleased to hear from you.
We do everything we can to provide the very latest information for your trip.

Nevertheless, despite all of our authors' thorough research, errors can creep in.
MARCO POLO does not accept any liability for this. Please contact us by e-mail or post.

MARCO POLO Travel Publishing Ltd
Pinewood, Chineham Business Park
Crockford Lane, Chineham
Basingstoke, Hampshire RG24 8AL
United Kingdom

PICTURE CREDITS

Cover Photograph: Dancing at the Rose Festival (Look: Wothe)
Images: Blickinsfreie: René Eckert (17 bottom); G. Diran (1 bottom); DuMont Bildarchiv: Schulze (3 bottom, 27, 48, 55, 90/91, 94/95, 104/105); R. Hackenberg (122/123); Huber: Schmid (flap l., 3 centre, 40/41, 44/45, 80/81); iStockphoto.com: zilli (16 top); Jürgens Photo (20); Laif: hemis.fr (74), Raach (2 centre bottom, 32/33, 66/67), Tophoven (12/13); Look: age fotostock (4), van Dierendonck (100/101), Wothe (1 top, 98/99); Markam Fashion: Alexander Nishkov (16 bottom); mauritius images: age (8), Alamy (2 top, 2 bottom, 5, 6, 9, 24/25, 26 l., 26 r., 37, 56/57, 68, 111), Handl (10/11), O'Brien (28); N-VISION Services Group Ltd.: TsvetelinaTsankova (17 top); R. Petrov (15, 106/107); Rakursi Art Gallery: Onnik Karanfilian (16 centre); D. Renckhoff (43, 53, 77, 89, 110 top, 110 bottom, 115); T. Stankiewicz (flap r., 30 l., 30 r., 60); Transit-Archiv: Schulze (2 centre top, 3 top,7, 18/19, 21, 22, 28/29, 29, 34, 39, 47, 51, 58, 63, 65, 71, 72/73, 76, 79, 82, 84/85, 86, 93, 96, 102, 104, 105, 106, 107)

1st Edition 2013

Worldwide Distribution: Marco Polo Travel Publishing Ltd, Pinewood, Chineham Business Park, Crockford Lane, Basingstoke, Hampshire RG24 8AL, United Kingdom. Email: sales@marcopolouk.com
© MAIRDUMONT GmbH & Co. KG, Ostfildern
Chief editors: Michaela Lienemann (concept, managing editor), Marion Zorn (concept, text editor)
Author: Magarditsch Hatschikjan; co-author: Galina Diran; Editor: Cordula Natusch
Programme supervision: Anita Dahlinger, Ann-Katrin Kutzner, Nikolai Michaelis
Picture editors: Gabriele Forst, Stefan Scholtz; What's hot: wunder media, Munich;
Cartography road atlas: © MAIRDUMONT, Ostfildern; Cartography pull-out map: © MAIRDUMONT, Ostfildern
Design: milchhof: atelier, Berlin; Front cover, pull-out map cover, page 1: factor product munich
Translated from German by Neil Williamson, Wilmslow; editor of the English edition: Paul Fletcher, Suffolk
Prepress: BW-Medien GmbH, Leonberg
Phrase book in cooperation with Ernst Klett Sprachen GmbH, Stuttgart, Editorial by Pons Wörterbücher

DOS & DON'TS ✋

A few things to bear in mind while in Bulgaria

DRIVING IN TOWN

Traffic in the major towns and cities is chaotic, especially in Sofia and Varna. The best thing to do is leave your car and hop on to public transport or take a taxi. But if you do decide to drive yourself, then it's best to park in a supervised car park – and absolutely not where there's any form of parking restriction. The Bulgarians don't hesitate, when it comes to towing cars away.

NODDING IN AGREEMENT

Situations where you have to make yourself understood by non-verbal means will be difficult to avoid. Therefore, so that you do not cause any misunderstandings, be aware that when Bulgarians nod, i.e. raise their head once and then move it slowly back down, that means 'No!' When they shake their head, i.e. move it left and then right and repeat it with vigorous agreement, that means 'Yes!' So, if you want to indicate to someone your non-verbal agreement – beware of nodding! In fact, the Bulgarian for 'yes' is 'da' and 'ne' for no, so it might be wise to use these instead of nodding or shaking your head.

BEING CARELESS

There's no need to panic, but you should still be very careful at all times. Be alert and keep a tight grip on all your valuables; make sure you park your car – even during the day – in supervised car parks; and don't leave cameras, handbags and other valuable items clearly visible in your car. And don't wander around with a large amount of cash on you. Mobile phones are often targeted by thieves, so take care when travelling in crowded buses and trams, especially in Sofia where there are often lots of pickpockets about.

GOING OUT FOR A WALK AT NIGHT

Beware of the dark! But it's not thieves who pose a threat to pedestrians, rather the potholes in the roads. So it's a good idea to take a torch with you to avoid this danger.

DEALING WITH BLACK MARKET TRADERS

It's not worth changing money on the street, and in any case it's illegal. Even though it happens less often than it used to, there are still some passers-by who approach tourists offering to change money. Usually the rate they're proposing is much better than the banks', but under no circumstances should you accept the offer, no matter how attractive it may look, because very skilled counterfeiters operate in Bulgaria. You also need to be careful, should you be asked to change high-value notes for smaller ones. Be on your guard in bureaux de change, some of which charge a high rate of commission. Always keep a close eye on your money and ask for a receipt; you can also ask for your money to be paid out in low-denomination notes to avoid any difficulties later with getting change. It's much, much safer to change money in a bank or, simplest of all, use a cash machine.